Refresh
My
Heart

in Spring

Published by Word Publishing, a division of
Thomas Nelson Inc., Nashville, Tennessee 37214

Compiled and edited by Terri Gibbs

Unless otherwise noted, all Scripture is from the New
King James Version. Copyright © 1979, 1980, 1982,
Thomas Nelson, Inc., Publishers.

J. Countryman is a registered trademark
of Word Publishing, Inc.

A J. Countryman Book

Designed by Left Coast Design Inc. Portland, Oregon.

ISBN 08499-5337-5

Contents

A woman feels a restlessness, a giddy, inexplicable aching in the spring. Old hopes rise from a long, long sleeping.

MARJORIE HOLMES

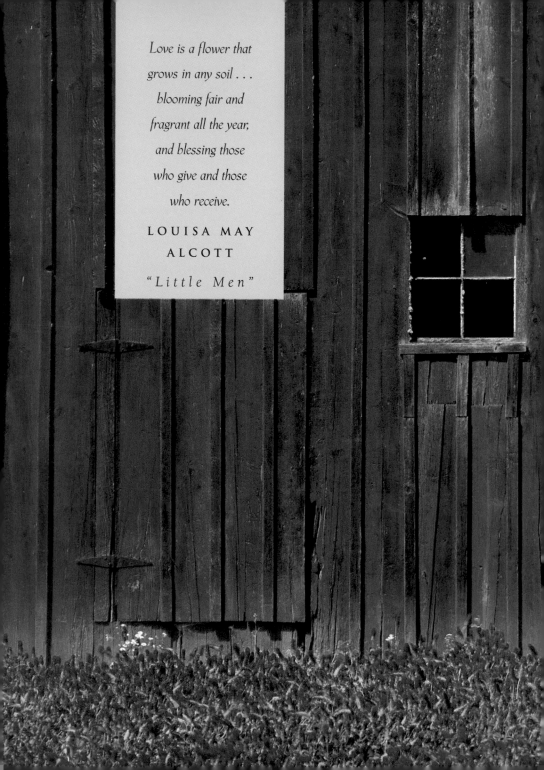

Love is a flower that
grows in any soil . . .
blooming fair and
fragrant all the year,
and blessing those
who give and those
who receive.

LOUISA MAY
ALCOTT

"Little Men"

A Well-Watered Garden

*By awesome deeds in righteousness
You will answer us, O God of our salvation.*

PSALM 65:5

pring is on its way in my garden. . . . Most plants have not yet begun to flower, and bulbs are just beginning to push up earth. The winter rains left plenty of large weeds behind. . . . I kneel and pull one weed at a time, carefully feeling at the base of each weed so as to pull it out by the roots. Grab, feel, pull. Grab, feel, pull. . . .

A garden soothes troubled hearts, delights the senses, feeds the body, and offers us a second Eden in which to play and rest. . . . Biblical writers, including Isaiah, used gardens as places of healing and enjoyment. Isaiah 58:11 promises healing and transformation to God's people when they behave justly toward their neighbors in need. And out of the desolation and devastation of a sun—scorched land the Lord will heal and strengthen the people, making them a well—watered garden, a source of life and nourishment to all who need them. Out of all of our pain and sorrow God creates in us a living garden of hope and healing. . . .

Amidst all our anxious striving with mortgages, kids, jobs, and life in general, God leads us to a garden and shows us a lily.

Time can never be brought back, and like money, it is spent one way or another.

EDITH
SCHAEFFER

Week 1

HARRIET CROSBY
A Place Called Home

Nothing can match
apple blossoms in spring,
pink–and–white flowers
lavishly piled on every branch,
as mouthwatering
as strawberries and cream.

FIONA MacMATH

Sunlight on Shattered Glass

*The LORD repay your work, and a full reward be given you by the
LORD God of Israel, under whose wings you have come for refuge.*

RUTH 2:12

My art studio is a mess of half-chewed pastel pencils, old tubes of paint, and piles of illustrations overflowing my file drawers. Recently while cleaning up, I discovered some broken glass on the counter by the window. I also discovered that when sunlight struck the shattered glass, brilliant, colorful rays scattered everywhere.

Shattered glass is full of a thousand different angles, each one picking up a ray of light and shooting it off in a thousand directions. That doesn't happen with plain glass, such as a jar. The glass must be broken into many pieces.

*If our faith is to be authentic
and personal, it must be tried
in the crucible of reality.*

PENELOPE J.
STOKES

What's true of shattered glass is true of a broken life. Shattered dreams. A heart full of fissures. Hopes that are splintered. A life in pieces that appears to be ruined. But given time and prayer, such a person's life can shine more brightly than if the brokenness had never happened. When the light of the Lord Jesus falls upon a shattered life, that believer's hopes can be brightened.

It's the nature of things that catch the light: The color and dazzle of light sparkles best through things that are shattered.

JONI EARECKSON TADA
Diamonds in the Dust

The Difficult Road of Faithfulness

❧

I will instruct you and teach you in the way you should go;
I will guide you with My eye.

PSALM 32:8

Did [Ruth] make a wrong decision in returning with Naomi to Bethlehem? She might have wondered, given the circumstances. In Moab, surely, her life would have been easier. At least she would have been among friends and family. Instead, she left everything familiar and chose a life of poverty and hardship.

Ruth was faithful to the path that was set before her. She committed herself to the decision and didn't second-guess God. And God gave her a second chance.

Not a second chance to reevaluate her path and return home, but an opportunity to see the faithfulness of the God of Israel displayed abundantly toward her. Ruth didn't know it when she set out on the difficult road of faithfulness, but something important was waiting for her in Bethlehem.

A God who loved her.

A husband.

A life.

PENELOPE J. STOKES
Faith: The Substance of Things Unseen

God's Hand In Mine

Love suffers long and is kind; love does not envy;
love does not parade itself, is not puffed up.

1 CORINTHIANS 13:4

When I lived in the forest of Ecuador, I usually traveled on foot. Except for one occasion when I went off alone (and quickly learned what a bad mistake that was), I always had with me a guide who knew the way or knew much better than I did how to find it. Trails often led through streams and rivers that we had to wade, but sometimes there was a log laid high above the water we had to cross.

Even as it is the nature of a seed to sprout, it is the nature of love to give itself away.

ROBERT
SCHULLER

I dreaded those logs and was always tempted to take the steep, hard way down into the ravine and up the other side. But the Indians would say, "Just walk across, senorita," and over they would go, confident and light-footed. I was barefoot as they were, but it was not enough. On the log, I couldn't keep from looking down at the river below. . . . So my guide would stretch out a hand, and the touch of it was all I needed. . . .

The lesson the Indians taught me was that of trust. The only thing I really needed, the touch of a steady hand, they could provide. . . .

I have found in the Bible plenty of evidence that God has guided people. I find, too, assurance that He is willing to guide me. He has been at it for a long time. His hand reaches toward me. I have only to take it.

ELISABETH ELLIOT
God's Guidance

This rule in gardening never forget, to sow dry and set wet.

OLD PROVERB

A Tiny Bit of Love

❧

Commit your way to the LORD, trust also in Him,
and He shall bring it to pass.

PSALM 37:5

*L*ove is a fruit always in season, and no limit is set. Everyone can reach this love.

Are we convinced of Christ's love for us and of our love for Him? This conviction is like the sun's rays, which cause the sap of life to flow and make the flowers of holiness blossom. This conviction is the rock on which holiness is built by serving Christ's poor and lavishing on them what we would love to do for Him in person.

If we follow this way, our faith will grow, our conviction will grow, and the striving for holiness will become our daily task. . . .

Perhaps only a smile, a little visit, or simply the fact of building a fire for someone, writing a letter for a blind person, bringing a few coals, finding a pair of shoes, reading for someone, this is only a little bit, yes, a very tiny bit, but it will be our love of God in action.

Our spiritual journeys are lived moment by moment, not day by day or even week by week.

LESLIE
WILLIAMS

❧

MOTHER TERESA
The Love of Christ

Notes

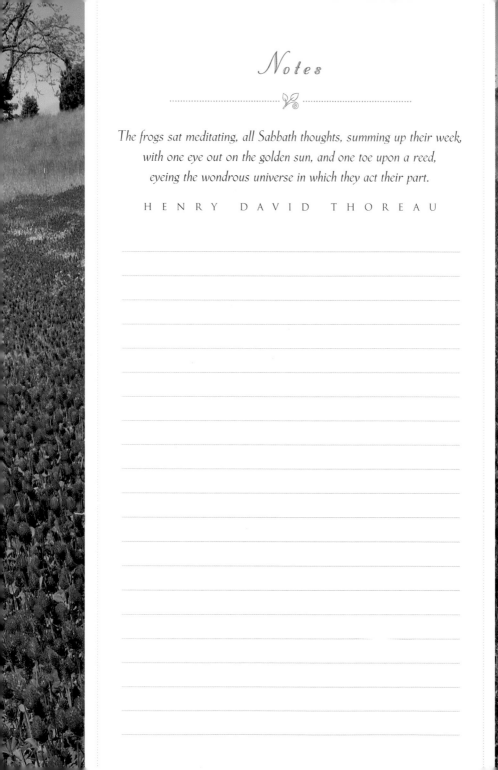

The frogs sat meditating, all Sabbath thoughts, summing up their week,
with one eye out on the golden sun, and one toe upon a reed,
eyeing the wondrous universe in which they act their part.

HENRY   DAVID   THOREAU

Behind the Clouds

*The LORD is a sun and shield; the LORD will give grace and glory;
no good thing will He withhold from those who walk uprightly.*

PSALM 84:11

My home is on a mountain nearly four thousand feet high. Many times we can see below us the clouds in the valley. Some mornings we wake up to find that we are in lovely sunshine, but the valley below is covered with clouds. At other times thunderstorms come up, and we can see the lightning flash and hear the thunder roar down below, while we are enjoying beautiful sunlight and clear skies above.

Many times I have sat on our rustic front porch and watched the clouds below. I have thought of the clouds of discouragement and suffering that temporarily veil the sunlight of God's love from us. Many people live with a cloud hanging over their lives. Some may be in hospital beds; others are suffering discouragement and bereavement. A heavy cloud hangs over them.

The Bible has a great deal to say about clouds, for they sometimes symbolize the spiritual forces which obscure the face of God. The Bible indicates that clouds are given to us for a purpose and that there is glory in the clouds and that every cloud has a silver lining.

God is in the details.

LUDWIG MIES
VAN DER ROHE

BILLY GRAHAM
Unto the Hills

For lo, the winter is past,

The rain is over and gone.

The flowers appear

on the earth;

The time of singing

has come.

SONG OF SOLOMON
2:11, 12

Beat the Blahs

*God is able to make all grace abound toward you, that you, always having
all sufficiency in all things, may have an abundance for every good work.*

2 CORINTHIANS 9:8

Here they come—those mid–March doldrums. It's that
time of year when spring makes several false starts, then a
"norther" blows in, catching peach trees at a popcorn stage,
so the chances of a good fruit crop lessen. Lima
beans refuse to sprout and our deacons refuse
to buy another cord of firewood, so we all
complain of cold feet at prayer meeting.

My grandmother never went out
and purchased a new hat to combat the
blahs. Money didn't grow on sassafras
bushes; and, besides, she preferred a
sunbonnet. But, oh yes, she had a cure.
"Let's do something impulsive!" she
used to say. . . .

Today, I looked back and tried to recall
some of the things we did—because they're
exactly what I plan to do!
1) Write a letter when it's
not your turn! 2) Call some
body you haven't heard from
in years; 3) Make a batch of

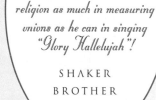

*A person can show his
religion as much in measuring
onions as he can in singing
"Glory Hallelujah"!*

SHAKER
BROTHER

Week 2

cookies and take them to a shut–in; and 4) Go out and look for a
stranger to smile at! None of these things cost a cent; but how long
has it been since I did them! So here goes.

JUNE MASTERS BACHER
Quiet Moments for Women

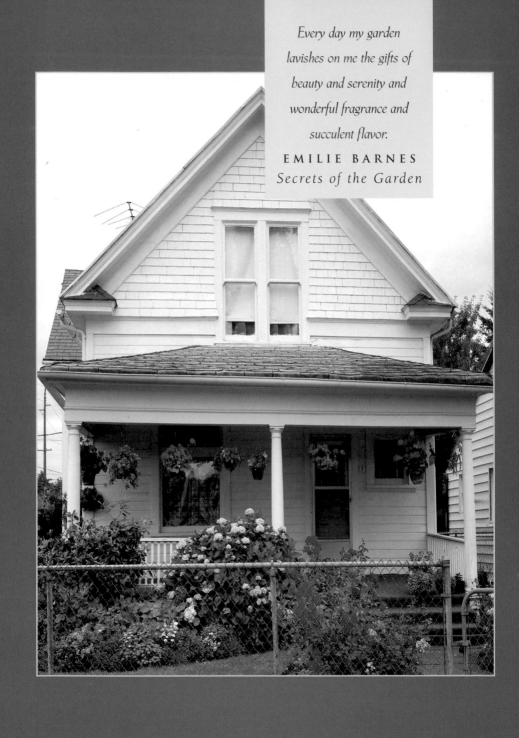

Every day my garden
lavishes on me the gifts of
beauty and serenity and
wonderful fragrance and
succulent flavor.

EMILIE BARNES
Secrets of the Garden

Beauty in God's Pattern

⁂

Whatever your hand finds to do, do it with your might. . . .

ECCLESIASTES 9:10

*G*od created. The Personal God who has always existed has always been creative. The evidence of His creativity we are able to see, day by day, all of our lives—the variety of notes in birdsongs. . . in woods, jungles, along lakeshores and mountain streams, and then we hear them copied in wind and string instruments.

Does the Bible rule out creativity as an unspiritual thing? Think of all of the marvelous things which God commanded to be made for the tabernacle, and for the Temple. The exact directions given to Moses for the tabernacle, and to Solomon for the Temple, included fantastic artworks—and meant that people needed to have the creative skills to produce these things.

It should not surprise us to read of the wonderful embroidery, silverwork, pure gold candlesticks, and bowls in these metals made with marvelous designs of almonds, with branches and flowers specified in the design. Someone had to weave the fine linen. Someone had to embroider with the "cunning work.". . . Someone made the veil for the Temple. Someone made the wonderful robes for the priests. Beauty, as well as spiritual meaning, was combined in God's given pattern.

It is certainly the Creator's will that the desires and talents He Himself has planted in us be realized.

CATHERINE
MARSHALL

⁂

EDITH SCHAEFFER
What Is a Family?

The Path We Tread

God has not given us a spirit of fear, but of power and of love and of a sound mind.

2 TIMOTHY 1:7

Our lives are like plotlines in a novel, with God as the Author. In literary terms, I have heard it said that there is no such thing as a Christian tragedy because, though tragic things may happen to the protagonist, the Christian always ends up in the arms of God. Death is not the last word. Disaster only brings the Christian closer to God. Nasty surprises or twists and turns of plot do not deter us from the path we tread. Because of the cross, we may march through earthly jungles, deserts, gardens, cities, but we are on a heavenly trek. No matter what our journeys lead us through, we always end up in God. From where we stand now, our future may look dreadful, exciting, boring, but we may rest assured that we are in better hands than our own if we simply give our future to Christ.

LESLIE WILLIAMS
Night Wrestling

Child-Faith

❧

In the fear of the LORD there is strong confidence,
and His children will have a place of refuge.

PROVERBS 14:26

*J*esus said, "I tell you the truth, unless you change and become like little children, you will never enter the kingdom of heaven" (Matthew 18:3).

It's not a threat. It's a principle.

Children trust. They are open and receptive and accepting. . . .

Children love. They give themselves unreservedly to those who have earned their respect and affection.

Children are wise. Instinctively, they can spot a phony in a second, but still they do not lose their childlike wonder, awe, and faith.

When Christ expresses the "child-faith" principle of entering the kingdom, I believe he refers to those attributes of childlikeness that balance our "adult" approach to life:

Questioning without cynicism.

Enthusiasm without concern for appearances.

Exploration without fear.

Failure without regret.

All of life is a gift, and God has given it for joy.

TERRY
LINDVALL

❧

PENELOPE J. STOKES
Faith: The Substance of Things Unseen

Fill the copper teakettle on
the summer-kitchen stove
and bring it just to the boil;
take from the oven the pans
of gingerbread. Serve the hot
and fragrant spicy tea from
an old Bennington teapot,
and enjoy a country tea
party in the spring.

MARY MASON
CAMPBELL

*The Butt'ry Shelf
Cookbook*

God's Gift of Each Day

❧

Let your gentleness be known to all men. The Lord is at hand.

PHILIPPIANS 4:5

Gradually as the sun moves in Grandeur across the sky, the hours of the day are flooded with light, warmed with pleasure. Then slowly as evening descends, the burning orb of fire settles softly into the sea, as though settling down gently for the night.

The brilliant banners of tattered clouds, tinged with intense red, rose, and pulsing scarlet hues, remind us that the day is done. What has been done has been done!

There can be no replay of this day, except in fleeting memory. There can be no rewriting of the script etched upon these hours. With the indelible ink of eternity there has been inscribed upon the page of this eternal sheet of time either something of value, or only what is vain.

If I look upon each day as a gift from God, how will I change? In what ways will my attitude alter and my perspective brighten? O Lord, help me to walk before You "blameless."

A quiet joy comes when we live the way God calls us to live.

JOHN YATES

❧

W. PHILLIP KELLER
Songs of My Soul

Notes

It is easy enough to be pleasant,
When life flows by like a song,
But the [woman] worth while is one who will smile,
When everything goes dead wrong.

ELLA WHEELER WILCOX

Trust and Glad Obedience

*Do not become sluggish, but imitate those who
through faith and patience inherit the promises.*

HEBREWS 6:12

*O God, holiness is a spark
from Thy love kindled
to a flame in my heart.*

PURITAN
PRAYER

Last evening as the sun went down a thick fog rolled in off the sea. I could see the dim shapes of the sea gulls in the midst of it, winging their way unerr—ingly west to Kettle Island, where they roost at night, guided by what the world calls "instinct," which is probably scientists' way of saying that they have no idea what guides them. I believe God guides them. Are they aware of it? Do the robin and the sparrow know they are cared for? We do not know. We do know there is a profound difference between them and us. We say "free as a bird," but the truth is God meant us to be freer than birds. He made us in His own image, which means He gave us things He did not give them: reason and will and the power to choose.

God calls me. In a deeper sense than any other species of earthbound creature, I am called. And in a deeper sense I am free for I can ignore the call. . . .

God created me with the power to disobey, for the freedom to obey would be nothing at all without the corresponding freedom to disobey. I can answer no, or I can answer yes. My fulfillment as a human being depends on my answer, for it is a longing Lord who calls me through the world's fog to His island of peace. If I trust Him, I will obey Him gladly.

ELISABETH ELLIOT
Discipline: The Glad Surrender

Spring lifts my heart.
Suddenly everything is in bloom.
I thrill at birds' songs
I missed all winter.

HARRIET CROSBY

A Well-Watered
Garden

The Nipping Frosts of Trials

························ ❧ ························

*It is good for me that I have been afflicted,
that I may learn Your statutes.*

PSALM 119:71

The crocuses in my backyard are fragrant and beautiful, even for the dry, warm climate of Southern California. I don't know how to account for such a profusion of flowers except to say that we had a couple weeks of hard frost back in January. I'm only an amateur gardener, but I'm convinced the freezing cold forced a lot of beauty out of my crocuses.

A theologian who also knew something about gardening once said, "The nipping frosts of trial and affliction are ofttimes needed if God's trees are to grow. They need the cold to revive and bud." What is true for crocuses is true for people.

It's interesting to note that David, who wrote our psalm for today, was not a hardheaded sort who needed to be pushed into line. He was not the type who required a little affliction in his life to get him to appreciate God. Rather, the psalmist was a man after God's own heart. But David's afflictions were not intended to mold him into shape. They were God's way of helping to create something beautiful in his life.

> *We are building lives with an eternal purpose in mind.*
>
> CHARLES STANLEY
>
> ❧

Week 3

JONI EARECKSON TADA
Diamonds in the Dust

One of the things I love
about Europe is the sight of
people rushing home for lunch
with a loaf of bread under
one arm and a fresh bouquet
in the other.

BARBARA MILO
OHRBACH
Simply Flowers

Big Wet Tears

❧

Those who sow in tears shall reap in joy.

PSALM 126:5

You can tell it's going to be a rotten day when
* you call suicide prevention and they put you on hold.
* you put your bikini top on backward and it fits better.
* your blind date turns out to be your ex-boyfriend.

But just remember, every flower that ever bloomed had to go through a whole lot of dirt to get there! And with the dirt, a lot of watering was needed. . . .

You don't have to grin and bear it. You don't have to be holier-than-thou, keeping up a "spiritual" front that equates tears with weakness and doubt. No, scientists now confirm what the Bible has said for thousands of years: tears are God's gift to his precious children. When we cry, we allow our bodies to function according to God's design—and we embrace one of the "perks" he offers to relieve our stress.

Sometimes, when we least expect it, a small cross proves a lovely crown.

LOUISA MAY
ALCOTT

❧

Someone said, "God will accept a broken heart, but he must have all the pieces." As he stitches those pieces back together, the moisture of tears softens and makes flexible his strong thread of healing in our lives. Big wet tears are part of the rich human experience. The people who weep unashamed are the same ones who live and love with their whole heart and soul.

BARBARA JOHNSON
Joy Breaks

A Well-Chosen Word

Let the words of my mouth and the meditation of my heart be acceptable in Your sight, O LORD, my strength and my Redeemer.

PSALM 19:14

A word fitly spoken," wrote the wise Solomon, "is like apples of gold in pictures of silver" (Prov. 25:11, KJV). Like Jell-O, concepts assume the mold of the words into which they are poured. Who has not been stabbed awake by the use of a particular word . . . or combinations of words? Who has not found relief from a well-timed word spoken at the precise moment of need? Who has not been crushed beneath the weight of an ill-chosen word? And who has not gathered fresh courage because a word of hope penetrated the fog of self-doubt? The word *word* remains the most powerful of all four-letter words.

Colors fade.

Shorelines erode.

Temples crumble.

Empires fall.

But "a word fitly spoken" endures.

CHARLES SWINDOLL
Simple Faith

Hold God's Hand in the Dark

*O LORD, you are the portion of my inheritance
and my cup; You maintain my lot.*

PSALM 16:5

*I*n my own pictorial view of seeking God's will I see a rushing stream in the mountains or fields, with stones big enough to put a foot on to cross. I picture God showing me one stone big enough to start across on, and then one stone on which to put my foot next. And then the waters whirl around, and I am to stay where I am, on that particular stone, until He shows me the next step. To rush ahead on my own would be disastrous. . . .

Heaven and earth are threads from one loom.

SHAKER
SAYING

It is a warning to watch out for impatience in wanting to "get on with it," whatever "it" happens to be. God tells us that to be in a fog, a dark place, to have no clue of what comes next, is to be in a place where we need to trust Him and keep our hand in His hand, waiting for Him to show us where to go or what to do next. . . .

All right—you and I often want to know, "What comes next?" God is saying, "Trust Me." He is saying, "Stay in the place where you are until I show you [in a variety of ways, usually not mystical at all] what comes next." He is saying, "Blessed is the person who waits in the dark, holding My hand."

EDITH SCHAEFFER
Common Sense Christian Living

I Choose Love

If we live in the Spirit, let us also walk in the Spirit.

GALATIANS 5:25

*I*t's quiet. It's early. My coffee is hot. The sky is still black. The world is still asleep. The day is coming. In a few moments the day will arrive. It will roar down the track with the rising of the sun. The stillness of the dawn will be exchanged for the noise of the day. The calm of solitude will be replaced by the pounding pace of the human race. The refuge of the early morning will be invaded by decisions to be made and deadlines to be met.

For the next twelve hours I will be exposed to the day's demands. It is now that I must make a choice. Because of Calvary, I'm free to choose. And so I choose.

I choose love . . .

No occasion justifies hatred; no injustice warrants bitterness. . . .

I choose joy . . .

I will invite my God to be the God of circumstance. . . .

I choose peace . . .

I will live forgiven. I will forgive so that I may live. . . .

Love, joy, peace, patience, kindness, goodness, faithfulness, gentleness, and self-control. To these I commit my day. If I succeed, I will give thanks. If I fail, I will seek his grace. And then, when this day is done, I will place my head on my pillow and rest.

The discipline of emotions is the training of responses.

ELISABETH ELLIOT

MAX LUCADO
When God Whispers Your Name

Notes

*Dear Lord Jesus, we shall have this day only once; before it is gone,
help us to do all the good we can, so that today is not a wasted day.*

STEPHEN GRELLET

1773 — 1855

A Friend for Every Situation

"I will be a Father to you, and you shall be My sons and daughters," says the LORD Almighty.

2 CORINTHIANS 6:18

We can well understand what an amazing experience it must have been for ordinary human beings to meet the Christ, who was totally truthful and absolutely honest. It was akin to stumbling on an oasis with clear bubbling springs of truth amid the dreadful desolation of a vast desert of dishonesty.

Is it any wonder that poor prostitutes, crude fishermen, ordinary children, and cunning tax collectors were captivated by Christ and came to consider Him their closest friend? But beyond all this, they learned to love Him dearly.

What happened then still happens today. When any person is prepared to come to Christ in open, honest humility, without pretense or sham, he at once finds a friend. There is an immediate response from our own inner spirit to the Spirit of truth apparent in the person of Jesus Christ. There is an attraction which is generated through our finding someone worthy of our utmost confidence and trust. There is nothing in life so calculated to relieve tension and strain as knowing there is a friend available to whom we can turn in every situation.

We don't have all the answers, but we do have God.

BARBARA JOHNSON

W. PHILLIP KELLER
Taming Tension

*I don't do what I do
because I aspire to
do wild and crazy and
wonderful things for God,
but because He draws me
into wild and crazy and
wonderful things
for His glory.*

BARB WOOLER

*(missionary to the
Pygmies of Africa)*

A Few Bumps Along the Way

❧

Trust in the LORD with all your heart,
and lean not on your own understanding.

PROVERBS 3:5

On our farm in Maryland, heavy rains were great for our furrowed fields, but disaster for the dirt road leading from the county highway to our farmhouse. Our truck would spin out on the wet earth, splattering gravel everywhere. The road was normally easy to drive, a straight line between our house and the highway. With rain, the road may have been straight, but it wasn't easy!

Journeying down that farm road is much like traveling the path ahead of you. When you trust in the Lord, He promises that the road will take you directly to the destination He plans. He will make your path straight, and you will arrive in His perfect timing. But your path, although straight, will not be smooth. It's direct, but you'd better expect storms along the way.

Don't be like the Israelites who, when they forgot about God, wandered around in circles for forty years. Their path to the Promised Land was anything but straight. Trust in the Lord, and He will take you directly to where He wants you to go. It's worth the few bumps, potholes, and uncomfortable places along the way.

Christ imparts more than a creed; He gives Himself.

HENRY
GARIEPY

❧

Week 4

JONI EARECKSON TADA
Diamonds in the Dust

The honeysuckle waits
    For Summer and for heat;
But violets in the chilly Spring
Make the turf so sweet.

CHRISTINA
ROSSETTI

Chosen

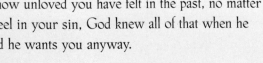

> *I give them eternal life, and they shall never perish;
> neither shall anyone snatch them out of My hand.*
>
> JOHN 10:28

*G*rafting is a nearly miraculous process in which one new plant is made out of two different ones. A branch is taken from one vine and inserted into a cut on another vine. The branch is bound to the new vine with an adhesive compound or tape. As the "wound" heals, the two plants become one, the new branch drawing sap from the roots of the established vine. . . .

Jesus told the disciples, "You did not choose me, but I chose you.". . .

Chosen. It's a humbling but comforting word.

Anyone who has ever waited in line only to be the last chosen for a team knows the terrifying humiliation of not being wanted. When we are grafted into Christ, we never have to know that humiliation again. There is no greater assurance than knowing that Jesus has chosen you and me to be grafted into him. Yet his choosing does not exclude anyone else. On this Vine there is room for everyone.

No matter how unloved you have felt in the past, no matter how lost you feel in your sin, God knew all of that when he chose you—and he wants you anyway.

WAYNE JACOBSEN
In My Father's Vineyard

*May I cherish simplicity
and godly sincerity
of character.*

PURITAN
PRAYER

It's Up to You

❧

Through God we will do valiantly, for it is
He who shall tread down our enemies.

PSALM 60:12

Have you ever heard of the story of the three negative women who lived in the bayou? They complained every day, "We've got it bad living in this bayou. No opportunity here. Others are living in the city where they have unlimited opportunities. Us, we got nothing." This is the complaint they lived their lives by, until one day a positive–thinking woman came along. After listening to the complaints, she said. "Nonsense! Opportunity? You want opportunity? You got opportunity. You live on the bayou. The bayou leads to the river. The river leads to the gulf. The gulf leads to the ocean. You can go anywhere from where you are!"

These are tough times you're going through, but if you're going to get through, it's up to you. Ready to go? Get ready to make your dreams come true!

ROBERT SCHULLER
Tough Times Never Last

God's Inexhaustible Strength

❧

*In the world you will have tribulation; but be
of good cheer, I have overcome the world.*

JOHN 16:33

Some days we outdo the eagles and rise above our circumstances, unconfined and unencumbered; we soar and see things from God's point of view. (Enjoy such moments!)

There are other days when, as the White Queen said to Alice, "it takes all the running you can to keep in the same place," or in the words of a plaque that used to hang over my mother's desk, the "hurrier you go the behinder you get." Those are the days we can maintain the pace with poise and persistence, sustained by God's inexhaustible strength.

*A joyful heart is a
normal result of a heart
that is burning
with love.*

MOTHER
TERESA

❧

And then there are those ordinary days when the desk is piled with dreary duties or the sink is full of dirty dishes and the routine is tedious and dull; when, as Ruth Bell Graham recalled, there's only "nothingness, inertia, skies gray and windless, no sun, no rain, no stab of pain, no strong regret, no reaching after, no tears, no laughter, no black despair, no bliss."

God delivers us through this. We can walk when the novelty has worn off, when the glory has faded, when the strength of youth is gone. This is the strength of God.

DAVID ROPER
Psalm 23

No matter how busy your life,
there should always be time
to pick a handful of whatever
flower is in perfect bloom
to put into the nearest jug
and proudly display on
kitchen tables, windowsills,
or church altars.

LAURA ASHLEY

God Uses Ordinary People

*God has chosen the weak things of the world to
put to shame the things which are mighty.*

1 CORINTHIANS 1:27

There is a recurring theme in Scripture about how the obscure, the weak, the ordinary, the *individual*, can have a profound effect on the whole. The Bible is a collection of individuals used by God to accomplish His expansive purposes in history. He seems to delight in affecting the many through the few. . . .

Consider a distraught Hannah in the temple, praying for a child so fervently that she appeared drunk. Think how she felt taking her only child—who was the answer to her many prayers—to live with a weak, indulgent old man, to be without the benefit of nursery school, swimming lessons, and (most of all) *her*. Hannah could not have known at that point that God would give her five more children and that the one she "gave away" would become perhaps the most godly, influential judge of Israel's history. What an incredible impact one life can make! . . .

God lays His hand upon the foolish, the weak, the base, and the despised to accomplish His purposes (1 Corinthians 1:26–29). He specializes in transforming those who could not into those who can.

*Those who bring sunshine
to the lives of others cannot
keep it from themselves.*

JAMES M.
BARRIE

STACY AND PAULA RINEHART
Living in Light of Eternity

Notes

Make your heart a lovely garden
Ever cautious what you sow;
Fill each space with seeds of kindness
So the deeds of God can grow.

JUNE   MASTERS   BACHER

Where Are the Lamps?

· ❧ ·

Let your light so shine before men, that they may see your good works and glorify your Father in heaven.

MATTHEW 5:16

*I*n a certain mountain village in Europe several centuries ago (so the story goes), a nobleman wondered what legacy to leave his townspeople. At last he decided to build them a church.

Nobody saw the complete plans until the church was finished. When the people gathered, they marveled at its beauty. But one noticed an incompleteness. "Where are the lamps?" he asked. "How will the church be lighted?"

The nobleman smiled. Then he gave each family a lamp. "Each time you are here, the area in which you sit will be lighted. But when you are not here, some part of God's house will be dark."

Today we live in a world of darkness, a darkness in which even our secular problem-solvers are beginning to stumble. In spite of our "social conscience," all around us is evidence of ignorance, illiteracy, and dark imaginings. . . .

The world is so big. And our lamp is so small. Yes, but we can light some small part each day.

O God, holiness is a spark from Thy love kindled to a flame in my heart.

PURITAN
PRAYER

❧

JUNE MASTERS BACHER
The Quiet Heart

It's a ratty little garden,

not much at all,

but I can call it mine.

KATHLEEN NORRIS

The Inner Garden

Great peace have those who love Your law,
and nothing causes them to stumble.

PSALM 119:165

I am a very results-oriented person. I like to be in control and make things happen—quickly! When I first planted my herb garden, I checked on its progress every day. I wanted immediate growth, immediate gratification. Of course, the more I demanded quick results from my garden, the less growth I saw. I could not see real growth when I obsessively measured each plant twice a day!

My herb garden taught me to take the long view of growth. It showed me that deep, lasting growth occurs slowly, over a long period of time. There is a difference between being obsessive and being faithful. Being faithful to my garden means tending and caring for it, providing the *conditions* for growth. I have no control over the results, the actual growth of my herbs. Like Paul, I plant. I water. But only God gives growth.

I learned the same lesson regarding my inner garden. I must be faithful—providing the *conditions* for spiritual growth by

> *To trust God completely requires the dicipline of surrender.*
>
> CHARLES SWINDOLL

Week 5

practicing the disciplines of prayer, Bible study, and worship. But it is God who brings about deep, lasting spiritual growth. And that takes a long time, often a lifetime.

HARRIET CROSBY
A Well-Watered Garden

The art of changing frowns
to smiles is never old–fashioned,
and lovely manners
smooth away the little worries
of life beautifully.

LOUIS MAY ALCOTT

"The Silver Party"

God's Great Gifts

God is my salvation and my glory; the rock of my strength.

PSALM 62:7

Almighty God, may my lips be a well-tuned harp to sound Thy praise.

PURITAN
PRAYER

Who of us has not responded happily and eagerly to the warmth and brightness of sunlight. How it stirs us in spring after the long, drab, cold days of winter. Even animals and plants, trees and birds respond to its touch and turn themselves toward its life–giving rays. All the world seems a brighter and better place to live when it is bathed in the beauty of sunlight. This is one of our Father's kind gifts to all His earthborn creatures. Without it, life on the planet would end abruptly. This golden, light–energy transmitted across millions of miles of subzero space enables photosynthesis to proceed on the earth. And this is the basis of all life.

We accept such a phenomenon as a matter of course, but in fact it is of such complexity that even the most erudite scientists cannot fully comprehend it. For those of us who are the children of God, we look up, lift up our hearts, and give thanks for so great a gift. It is to us another demonstration of our Father's care and provision for us as His people.

W. PHILLIP KELLER
A Shepherd Looks at the Good Shepherd and His Sheep

The Holy Spirit, Our Teacher

❧

I will dwell in them and walk among them.
I will be their God, and they shall be My people.

2 CORINTHIANS 6:16

As a child in the second or third grade, I was having trouble with arithmetic. I tried very hard in school to understand, and I did my homework diligently every night, often asking my father to explain things I had missed in class. But the lessons were so hard for me that I lay awake at night crying for fear I would fail. One day the teacher said, "If there is anything you don't understand, ask me. That's what I'm here for, you know."

I shall never forget the enormous relief that simple statement brought to me. It had never occurred to me, and I suppose she thought it was so obvious to us she didn't need to say it, but the logic of it hit me: that *was* what she was there for. Why else was she called a teacher? And she was there to teach *me.*

God has given us a teacher. That is why we have the Holy Spirit. "When the Spirit of truth comes, he will guide you into all the truth" [John 16:3 RSV]. "If any of you lack wisdom, let him ask of God" [James 1:5].

ELISABETH ELLIOT
God's Guidance

I Do Ask

*So I will strengthen them in the LORD, and they
shall walk up and down in His name.*

ZECHARIAH 10:12

Lord Jesus, You who were born in a stable
and laid in the straw, You who walked dusty
roads and were thirsty, and relished the
feel of cool water sliding down Your throat, and
laughed, and sometimes cried salty tears—You
are the One summoning me back to reality. I see
it now—what I have considered lofty spirituality
is sham and humbug in Your eyes. Worse than
that, often it has been a cloak to hide my fear of
not receiving what I ask You for.

*Faith untried is simply a
promise and a possibility—
tried faith is pure gold.*

OSWALD
CHAMBERS

You who are so much more alive than I am, now
want to go with me down the city street and help me
find a parking place, and remind me where I misplaced
that slip of paper with the telephone number. You want to
give my wife a good night's sleep, to heal my neighbor's
arthritis, to help John find a job. Happiness floods my heart at the
knowledge of Your being *Man* as well as God; the essence of any
difficulty I ever encounter, You have experienced before me.

So You are bidding me tell You my every need and promising
that joy and good gifts await my asking.

CATHERINE MARSHALL
Adventures in Prayer

It is exalting,
delicious to stand embraced
by the shadows of a
friendly tree with the wind
at your coat–tail and the
heavens hailing your heart,
to gaze and glory and give
oneself again to God.

JIM ELLIOT

Crown of Splendor

⸎

The eyes of the LORD are on the righteous,
and His ears are open to their prayers.

1 PETER 3:12

When Ken and I were in Russia, we befriended an old woman who cleaned the floors of our hotel lobby every day. Through an interpreter, we complimented her on doing an excellent job. Old and wrinkled, her round and red cheeks were framed with a tightly knotted colorful scarf. Her face sparkled with her blue eyes and golden-toothed smile. She had on layers of skirts and wore leggings and boots. With broom in hand, our elderly friend looked out of place in the hotel lobby; maybe that's why we were drawn to her.

The flow of prayer is like the Gulf Stream, imparting warmth to all that is cold.

ABRAHAM JOSHUA
HESCHEL

⸎

We met many Russian "babushkas" like her. The praying grandmothers, they were called. These were the stalwart saints of whom Stalin had cruelly said, "If we can get rid of these old women, we will have the youth in our grasp."

Stalin failed. And thank God for praying grandmothers who served as a link, spanning a generation lost to atheism and connecting a new generation of young people who are asking open, honest questions about Jesus.

How grateful we can be to elderly saints who make prayer a life vocation.

JONI EARECKSON TADA
Diamonds in the Dust

Notes

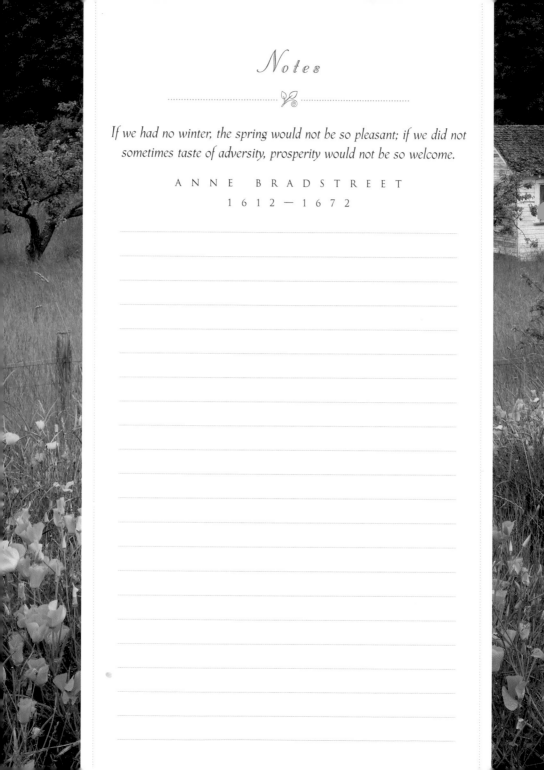

If we had no winter, the spring would not be so pleasant; if we did not sometimes taste of adversity, prosperity would not be so welcome.

ANNE BRADSTREET
1612 — 1672

Life Without End

So then faith comes by hearing, and hearing by the word of God.

ROMANS 10:17

At the end of his great book *Fathers and Sons*, Ivan Turgenev describes a village graveyard in one of the remote corners of Russia.

Among the many neglected graves was one untouched by man, untrampled by beast. Only the birds rested upon it and sang at daybreak. Often from the nearby village two feeble old people, husband and wife, moving with heavy steps and supporting one another, came to visit this grave.

Kneeling down at the railing and gazing intently at the stone under which their son was lying, they yearned and wept. After a brief word they wiped the dust away from the stone, set straight a branch of a fir tree, and then began to pray. In this spot they seemed to be nearer their son and their memories of him. And then Turgenev asks, "Can it be that their prayers, their tears, are fruitless? Can it be that love, sacred, devoted love, is not all powerful? Oh no, however passionate, sinning and rebellious the heart hidden in the tomb, the flowers growing over it peep serenely at us with their innocent eyes. They tell us not of eternal peace alone, of that great peace of indifferent nature; they tell us, too, of eternal reconciliation and of life without end."

Ultimately, hope will not disappoint us.

OSWALD
CHAMBERS

BILLY GRAHAM
Unto the Hills

There was a warm touch
of spring in the air as I
climbed the ridge. . . . The
evergreens were tipped
with vivid green, and the
willows overhanging the streams
were a whisper of green lace.

CATHERINE
MARSHALL

Christy

I always love the look
of white tulips
in a big silver vase
or overblown lilacs in an old
blue-and-white pitcher.

**BARBARA MILO
OHRBACH**

Simply Flowers

Quiet Adoration

The LORD is good to those who wait for
Him, to the soul who seeks Him.

LAMENTATIONS 3:25

Whenever I am afield or outdoors, there steals over me the acute consciousness that I am confronted on every hand by the superb workmanship of my Father. It is as if every tree, rock, river, flower, mountain, bird, or blade of grass had stamped upon it the indelible label, "Made by God." Is it any wonder that in a simple yet sublime sense of devotion, respect, and reverence for all of life, Christ longed for His Father's name to be hallowed throughout the earth. After all it is His realm. . . .

We demand God's gifts to satisfy our cravings. Yet, only His presence can do the trick.

LESLIE
WILLIAMS

As I pen these lines, it is a sun-dappled day in the lovely lake country of British Columbia. The high hills across the lake lie in their own deep blue shadows. Cloud patterns drift across the wind-stirred waters. The call of wild Canadian geese is borne above the shore cliffs on the breeze. And all around, green grass springs from soil warmed by April's sunshine. Man and all his inventions have had no part in producing a single

Week 6

one of these glorious sensations. All of them have come directly from the creative hand of my Father in heaven. Little marvel I often bow my heart in quiet adoration and gratitude to whisper, "How great Thou art!"

W. PHILLIP KELLER
A Shepherd Looks at the Good Shepherd and His Sheep

God handed me a morning
All freshly-dipped in dew;
I said, "How shall I use it?"
He said, "It's up to you."

JUNE MASTERS
BACHER

The Hard Makes It Good

············ ✧ ············

He will not allow your foot to be moved;
He who keeps you will not slumber.

P s a l m   1 2 1 : 3

*I*n the blockbuster comedy *A League of Their Own*, Dottie, the star catcher and hitter, decides to bail out on her team when her husband returns from World War II. She tells her coach, "I can't do it anymore. It's just too hard."

And the coach replies, "Of course it's hard. It's supposed to be hard. If it was easy, anybody could do it. The hard is what makes it good."

Consider your own life: spiritual, professional, personal. Chances are, the memorable times in your life, the experiences that brought growth and development, were the times of taking chances, of facing a difficult challenge and overcoming it.

Quitting a dead-end job and taking the risk to find more meaningful work.

Laboring for months—years, even—to overcome a thorny problem in your marriage.

Hanging in there with a rebellious teenager and finally rejoicing when he turns his life around. . . .

These are the moments of glory, the times when all the difficulty, all the stress, all the struggle, all the pain, are transformed. . . .

And we realize that only the difficult stuff is really worthwhile.

When our future is foggy or fuzzy, the Lord is our only hope.

CHARLES
SWINDOLL

✧

P E N E L O P E   J .   S T O K E S
Faith: The Substance of Things Unseen

God's Love Is Always Aware

················· ✣ ·················

As the Father loved Me, I also have loved you; abide in My love.

JOHN 15:9

*E*ven as I write, I see from my window a baby rabbit dart out from the underbrush, followed by the mother. She chases him in a circle for a minute, so fast it looks as though they forget who is chasing whom. Suddenly they both disappear into the underbrush. A minute later a young woodchuck waddles out, vacuums the grass slowly with his black snout, and waddles back. . . .

And are we not of much greater value than many sparrows or bunnies or woodchucks? The life and death of all of us is in the same Hands. We are always surrounded by the Unseen, among whom are the angels, ministers of fire, explicitly commissioned to guard us. He who keeps us neither slumbers nor sleeps. His love is always awake, always aware, always surrounding and upholding and protecting. If a spear or a bullet finds its target in the flesh of one of His servants, it is not because of inattention on His part. It is because of love.

ELISABETH ELLIOT
The Path of Loneliness

A Gallery of Memories

· ✦ ·

Teach me to do Your will, for You are my God; Your Spirit is good.

PSALM 143:10

Our past is like an art gallery. Walking down those corridors of our memory is like walking through an art gallery. On the walls are all of yesterday's pictures: our home, our childhood, our parents, our rearing, the heartaches, the difficulties, the joys and triumphs as well as the abuses and the inequities of our life. Since Jesus Christ our Lord is the same yesterday and today and forever, then we can take the Christ of today and walk with Him into our yesterday and ask Him to remove the pictures that bring bad or defeating memories. In other words, the Christian can let Jesus invade yesterday and deal with those years of affliction—those years which the locusts have eaten (Joel 2 :25–26)—and remove those scenes from the corridors of our lives. I have them. You have them. We need to let Him leave the murals that bring pleasure and victory and take down from the walls those things that bring despair and defeat.

Only forgiveness frees hurt people to pursue the character of Christ with any hope of success.

ANDY
SIANLEY

✦

CHARLES SWINDOLL
David: A Man of Passion and Destiny

Awake, O north wind,
and come, O south!
Blow upon my garden,
that its spices may flow out.

SONG OF
SOLOMON 4:16

Open Wounds, Closed Chapters

❧

God is our refuge and strength, a very present help in trouble.

PSALM 46:1

I was in the Kansas City airport waiting for my flight home when a family sat in the gate area near me. There were five of them—a small boy and girl, their mother and grandparents. The children were going to visit their father for the summer, they told me, fulfilling the terms of the new custody agreement. This would be their first summer away.

I watched as the mother cleverly turned away from adjusting the children's sweaters and backpacks just in time to intercept her own persistent tears. Their grandfather, who appeared rugged and hard-working, occasionally lifted a callused hand to discreetly brush his cheek. . . .

Open wounds. Closed chapters. Divided loyalties. It is no wonder it hurts so much. . . .

Jesus knew there would be stretches of our journey when nothing made sense. He knew lanes would end without warning. He knew life would often demand that we drink from sorrow's cup—one healthy dose after another. . . .

It is a good thing, that Jesus was "a man of sorrows, and acquainted with grief . . ." (Isaiah 53:3 KJV). It is good that He understands just how painful endings can be.

JANET PASCHAL
The Good Road

If I weep at night, give me joy in the morning.

PURITAN PRAYER

❧

Notes

The walled garden is an ancient symbol of the
soul—precious, secret, known only to God.

FIONA MACMATH

The God Who Sees

*The slave girl gave a name to the LORD who spoke
to her: "You are 'God-who-sees-me.'"*

GENESIS 16:13 NCV

Hagar, the pregnant maidservant of Sarah, had fled into the wilderness. She just wanted to die. But God sent an angel who found her and told her to go back home even though it was the hardest place to go. He then predicted that the child born to her would be a wild man who wouldn't get along with anybody.

Now I don't know about you, but if I were Hagar, that's not exactly what I would have wanted to hear. Hagar's response, however, was to call God a name that had never been used before: *The-God-Who-Sees.* And she accepted what he said.

'When a lifestorm has left our way treacherous, we need God to guide us through.

VERDELL
DAVIS

Yes, our God is the all-knowing One who sees our scars, our secrets, and our strength. Our wounds and shame are his affair, and he knows just how much trouble we can stand. Somehow, the fact that he knows us so well makes a difference. We understand there is a direction, and we are part of a bigger picture. From the wildernesses in our lives, the fact that *he sees* gives us a reason to carry on. No longer are we anonymous, lonely, and lost.

BARBARA JOHNSON
Joy Breaks

The tea and cookies joined a
hodgepodge of cups and saucers
on an oval golden oak tea tray
made by Papa, along with
a sugar bowl, a small pitcher
of milk, [and] lemon slices. . . .
Nothing matched, all was
serviceable. . . . It was homely
in the best way: think of
Little Women and you've got it.

HELEN GUSTAFSON

*The Agony of the
Leaves*

The Life of the Lily

✿

Most assuredly, I say to you, he who believes in Me has everlasting life.

JOHN 6:47

The flower known today as "lily of the valley" is a harbinger of spring. Like the crocus, it peeks its fragrant head through the hard ground and softening snow and tells us, "Winter is over and spring has come!" Its creamy white flowerets speak of purity; its bright green leaves are symbolic of life. . . .

The most famous lily, the madonna lily, has been around some three millennia. Its bulbs were found in the sarcophagi of ancient Egyptian mummies. The pure white lily we see at weddings and funerals today took on its greatest role as the symbol of Mary, the mother of Jesus. In honor of her and the Son she bore, lilies began appearing everywhere in Christian art, and so the connection began in earnest.

God's greatest work has never been done in crowds, but in closets.

GEORGE
MACDONALD

Jesus himself waved his arm at a field of beautiful lilies and said, ". . . even Solomon in all his glory was not arrayed like one of these" (Matt. 6:29). . . .

Even the tiny flowers we know as the lily of the valley remind me of my Savior because he, too, represents purity and life, a fragrant sacrifice, a harbinger of new life after cold death.

LIZ CURTIS HIGGS
Reflecting His Image

Week 7

*Spring comes as subtly
as snow in the night. It slips
up on you with its vague
powderings of green. . . . The
ground is suddenly brash
with grass, the forsythias leap
into yellow flame.*

MARJORIE HOLMES

Lord, Let Me Love

The Crazy Quilt of Friendship

············· ❧ ·············

You are my friends if you do whatever I command you.

JOHN 15:14

Recently my family relocated to a new town, and I was in bed with the flu, wrapped in my great-grandmother's crazy quilt. I felt sorry for myself, and I missed the friends I'd left behind. Deep down, I knew it was partly my own fault—I hadn't taken steps to establish new friendships. Several acquaintances seemed willing, but I was holding back, hesitating. . . .

As I studied the crazy quilt, I thought of the many friends I'd had throughout my life. Some felt a bit scratchy and rough like a sturdy piece of wood, but in time they softened—or I became used to them. Others were delicate like silk and needed to be handled with care. Some were colorful and bright and great fun to be with. . . .

Many of my friends have only been around for a season. So often I've had to leave them behind, or they leave me! And yet, in my heart, I know they are friends for life. . . .

And that's because God has sewn them into my heart.

I pulled the old quilt closer around me, comforted and warmed by my memories. Surely, my own masterpiece—this quilt of friendships I fretted over—was not nearly finished. I *would* make new friends in this town.

The only condition for loving is to love without conditions.

BARBARA
JOHNSON

❧

MELODY CARLSON

Patchwork of Love

The Trojan Horse of Bitterness

⁂

*Let all bitterness, wrath, anger, clamor, and evil speaking
be put away from you, with all malice.*

EPHESIANS 4:31

A Trojan horse sits just outside the gate of your heart. Its name is bitterness. It is a monument to every attack you have endured from your fellow human beings. It is a gift left by the people who have wronged you. It is a monument to the pain, the sorrow, and the devastation they have caused you. It represents the debt they will owe you until the day they are brought to justice. It is rightfully yours.

But to accept the gift is to invite ruin into your life. You see, there is more to the horse than meets the eye. The feeling of justification it brings is the deceptive artistry of a master craftsman. Though decorated with the promise of vindication, it is only a lure. The celebration is short-lived. Once inside the walls of your heart, it releases its agents of destruction. Its plot quietly unfolds from the inside out. To become a person of character, you must learn to recognize the Trojan horse of bitterness. And more important, you must *never* bring it inside.

ANDY STANLEY
Like a Rock

Work Done for Christ

------------ ✣ ------------

You open Your hand and satisfy the desire of every living thing.

PSALM 145:16

There is no such thing as Christian work. That is, there is no work in the world which is, in and of itself, Christian. Christian work is any kind of work, from cleaning a sewer to preaching a sermon, that is done by a Christian and offered to God.

This means that nobody is excluded from serving God. It means that no work is "beneath" a Christian. It means there is no job in the world that needs to be boring or useless. A Christian finds fulfillment not in the particular kind of work he does, but in the way in which he does it. Work done for Christ all the time must be "full-time Christian work.". . .

All work performed honorably before God is holy.

CLAIRE
CLONINGER

✣

Interest and challenge can always be found in any task done for God. If our work seems to be beneath us, if it becomes boring and meaningless, mere drudgery, it may be a living, but it is not living. It is not the life of freedom and fullness a disciple's life is designed to be.

Does God ask us to do what is beneath us? This question will never trouble us again if we consider the Lord of heaven taking a towel and washing feet.

ELISABETH ELLIOT
Discipline: The Glad Surrender

Spring is God's way
of celebrating, of telling
the world how much
He loves all of creation.

HARRIET CROSBY

The Road Home

❧

Return to the LORD your God, for He is gracious and
merciful, slow to anger, and of great kindness.

JOEL 2:13

*I*t was a warm Saturday afternoon. A Carolina breeze was steadily moving through the long grass and the proud, full branches. I was driving home, back to the little corner of the world where I grew up. I was en route to a modest house on a corner lot bordered by pine trees, vegetable gardens, and neighbors who still bake casseroles for each other.

I was thinking that when I arrive, my dad (most likely atop his newly painted tractor) will head across the freshly mown lawn. He'll hug me long and hard until the back door slams. My mom will reach for me, smiling, and announce, "I've a fresh pitcher of iced tea. Who's ready for a glass?" . . .

What really matters is home This is the stuff I am made of: This is what is important to me.

We are all on a homeward journey. God patiently plans our routes and polices our perils. He watches us maneuver through detours and treacherous places. He even sees us make an occasional wrong turn then keep going anyway.

But always He waits. Long ago He paved the way and marked the direction for us to come to Him. He prepared a place of rest that is beyond the reaches of our imaginations—a welcome center built by His own hand.

The Bible is the road map back to God.

JOEL GREGORY

JANET PASCHAL
The Good Road

Notes

On Easter Day the lilies bloom,
Triumphant, risen from their tomb;
Their bulbs have undergone rebirth,
Born from the silence of the earth—
Symbolically—to tell all men
That Christ, the Savior, lives again. . . .

JUNE MASTERS BACHER

The Tunnel of Testing

*The LORD raises those who are bowed down;
the LORD loves the righteous.*

PSALM 146:8

*Let every trial teach
me more of Thy peace,
more of Thy love.*

PURITAN
PRAYER

Someone has said that if one suffers without succeeding, he can be sure that the success will come in someone else's life. If he succeeds without suffering, he can be equally sure that someone else has already suffered for him.

After sixteen difficult years as a missionary on the continent of Africa, David Livingstone returned to his native Scotland to address the students at Glasgow University. His body was emaciated by the ravages of some twenty-seven fevers that had coursed through his veins during the years of his service. One arm hung useless at his side, the result of being mangled by a lion. The core of his message to those young people was "Shall I tell you what sustained me amidst the toil, the hardship, and loneliness of my exile? It was Christ's promise, 'Lo, I am with you always, even unto the end.'"

We, like David Livingstone, may claim the same promise from our Savior and Lord. He *does* go with us through our sufferings, and He awaits us as we emerge on the other side of the tunnel of testing—into the light of His glorious presence to live with Him forever!

BILLY GRAHAM
Unto the Hills

Friends and flowers
both are to be treasured.
And when it comes to
expressions of our affection
for special friends . . . I think
that flowers are
the nicest thing we can give.

**BARBARA MILO
OHRBACH**

Simply Flowers

Newness of Life

❧

Stand still and consider the wondrous works of God.

JOB 37:14

The almond trees have come alive! Their branches are strung with feathery, pink blossoms. The air is loud with bees. A spring–sweet perfume—light and elusive—rises up to greet the new season. The scene, so Genesis–fresh, brings with it the promise of harvest. This is what my grandmother would have referred to as a "fruitful spring."

I look upon those old almond trees (they are the senior citizens of the orchards in temperate climates) and wonder who planted the kernels and who grafted or budded the sweet–almond branches onto the bitter almond stock. . . .

As a child I used to think that spring happened suddenly. Now, I know that spring emerges gradually, as new as dawn—and as old. And inside our hearts there is a newness of life and an oldness of promise. We, like the trees, will emerge triumphantly as we allow our Creator to graft the sweet wood of faith onto our bitter stock.

The happiest people on this earth are those who are doing the most for other people.

C. A.
ROBERTS

Week 8

JUNE MASTERS BACHER
The Quiet Heart

This day is a gift
from the outflung hand of God;
The gift of an untrod road
for our feet to tread.

GRACE NOLL
CROWELL

No Other Way

· 🌿 ·

We ought to obey God rather than men.

ACTS 5:29

*I*n order to get to a place called Laity Lodge in Texas you have to drive into a riverbed. The road takes you down a steep, rocky hill into a canyon and straight unto the water. There is a sign at the water's edge which says, "Yes. You drive in the river."

One who has made up his mind to go to the uttermost with God will come to a place as unexpected and perhaps looking as impossible to travel as that riverbed looks. He may glance around for an alternative route, but if he wants what God promises His faithful ones, he must go straight into the danger. There is no other way.

The best way I know to face each day is to prepare the heart first thing in the morning.

RAVI ZACHARIAS

🌿

The written word is our direction. Trust it. Obey it. Drive in the river and get to Laity Lodge. . . .

When you take the risk of obedience, you find solid rock beneath you—and markers, evidence that someone has traveled this route before. "The Lord your God will cross over at your head . . . he will be with you; he will not fail you or forsake you. Do not be discouraged or afraid" (Deuteronomy 30:19, 20; 31:3, 8, NEB).

ELISABETH ELLIOT
Keep a Quiet Heart

Nothing Is Too Small

⁓

*My God shall supply all your need according
to His riches in glory by Christ Jesus.*

PHILIPPIANS 4:19

God created snowflakes, no two of which are alike. He created a spongelike pad between the head of a woodpecker and its bill to absorb the shock when the bird strikes a tree. He created small barbs along the feathers of each bird—as many as one million barbs per feather!—that act like zippers to lock the feathers together, not only waterproofing the bird but enabling it to catch air under its wings so that it can fly. He created seventy-five thousand miles of blood vessels in the human body that carry blood to over sixty trillion cells! More than one million of these cells are white antibodies, each one designed to fight just one kind of germ or virus. . . .

God is active in small ways in the universe, on our planet, in our bodies, and in our lives! What do you think is so small that it's *too* small for God to notice?

A small tear? A small hurt feeling?

A small kindness? A small insult?

A small sin? . . .

A small worry that is robbing you of your joy?

Nothing is too small for the Creator's attention and activity!

ANNE GRAHAM LOTZ
The Glorious Dawn of God's Story

Sweep Away the Cobwebs

*Our light affliction, which is but for a moment, is working
for us a far more exceeding and eternal weight of glory.*

2 CORINTHIANS 4:17

Growing up on a farm was one big adventure
for me. My sisters and I would jump from
barn rafters, build hay forts, and crawl
into the feed bin. I'd shinny up the ladder to the
hayloft, climbing through layers of thick cobwebs
that hung like cotton candy strung from one post
to another.

Spiders didn't bother me back then, so I
thought nothing of barging through their webs.
The thin threads clung to me, but I laughed—with
a sweep of my hand, the cobwebs were gone.

Someone once prayed, "Lord, help us to strip off
like cobwebs the troubles that we have allowed to cling
to us like chains." Oh, how often we feel chained to our
problems. Wouldn't it be glorious if we could consider all our
trials to be as light and as momentary as cobwebs? We can!
Whatever troubles are weighing you down—doubt or anxiety,
insecurity or fears—are not chains. They are featherweight
when compared to the glory yet to come. With a sweep of a
prayer and the praise of a child's heart, God can strip away
any cobweb.

*No sin is great enough to
drain dry the ocean
of God's grace.*

ELISABETH
ELLIOT

JONI EARECKSON TADA
Diamonds in the Dust

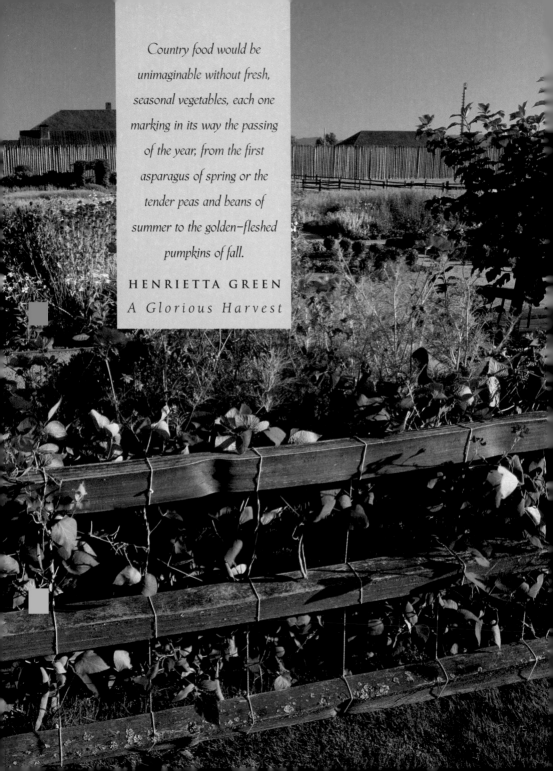

Country food would be
unimaginable without fresh,
seasonal vegetables, each one
marking in its way the passing
of the year, from the first
asparagus of spring or the
tender peas and beans of
summer to the golden–fleshed
pumpkins of fall.

HENRIETTA GREEN
A Glorious Harvest

Just Keep Pedaling

·· ❧ ··

Great is our LORD, and mighty in power; His understanding is infinite.

PSALM 147:5

When I learned to ride a bicycle, I did it badly—at least in comparison to other neighborhood kids. I had no sense of balance. I'd wobble and roll, wibble and rock. I ended up with scraped knees and shins. . . .

Fortunately, a neighborhood friend offered to teach me how to ride. He seemed so confident. "It's simple," he said. "The problem is you haven't got enough momentum going to keep in balance. Once you get going fast enough long enough you won't have any trouble at all. . . .

In the kingdom of God, there are days we think we'll never learn our lesson because circumstances are too overwhelming. We view difficult circumstances as threats, not opportunities. We think they are going to hurt (and they might). We want to grow up and do exciting things like the other kingdom kids, but we don't want to bloody our knees and shins in the process.

Then the Holy Spirit whispers, "Come on, I'll teach you. I'll show you how to use momentum to get where God wants you to go with your life." The Holy Spirit knows we have what it takes to keep upright once we're shoved ahead. Yes, there are lots of wobbles along the way and more than a few dangers. But with time we learn to assume control over those things—if we just keep pedaling.

Although self-control comes from the Spirit of God, we actively carry it out.

CHARLES R. SWINDOLL

❧

BARBARA JOHNSON
Joy Breaks

Notes

In some good time, His good time, I shall arrive:
He guides me and the bird. In His good time.

ROBERT   BROWNING
1 8 1 2 — 1 8 8 9

God, Our Father

❧

Remember, O LORD, Your tender mercies and
Your lovingkindnesses, for they are from of old.

PSALM 25:6

Recently, my daughter Jenna and I spent several days in the old city of Jerusalem .... One afternoon, as we were exiting the Jaffa gate, we found ourselves behind an orthodox Jewish family—a father and his three small girls. One of the daughters, perhaps four or five years of age, fell a few steps behind and couldn't see her father. *"Abba!"* she called to him. He stopped and looked. Only then did he realize he was separated from his daughter. *"Abba!"* she called again. He spotted her and immediately extended his hand. . . .

He held her hand tightly in his as they descended the ramp. . . . When the signal changed, he led her and her sisters through the intersection. In the middle of the street, he reached down and swung her up into his arms and continued their journey.

Isn't that what we all need? An *abba* who will hear when we call? Who will take our hand when we are weak? Who will guide us through the hectic intersections of life? Don't we all need an *abba* who will swing us up into his arms and carry us home? We all need a father.

God can take your trouble and change it into treasure.

BARBARA JOHNSON

❧

MAX LUCADO
The Great House of God

A cloud of lovely
yellow butterflies flew up
from a wild-rose bush,
and went dancing away higher
and higher, till they vanished
in the light beyond the wood.

LOUISE MAY
ALCOTT

"The Skipping Shoes"

A Song of Praise for Spring

*Praise the name of the LORD your God,
who has dealt wondrously with you.*

JOEL 2:26

This is just a little song of praise for spring, Lord, and the wonders it works in me. The way it makes me want to rearrange things, clean and decorate things— the house, the garden, myself!

It's as if your sunshine, spilling across the waking earth, spills through a woman's spirits too. Why else should I feel this mad urge to paint the bathroom (forsythia yellow), tidy up closets and cupboards, add more purple cushions of creeping phlox to the driveway? . . .

Best of all, Lord, spring inspires me to do some neglected housecleaning and refurbishing of my spirit.

Out with self-pity, old grudges, regrets. In with self-esteem . . . To refresh my own interior with a new supply of forgiveness and understanding, of goals and delights and dreams. To scatter these like seeds in the soil of myself and literally feel them grow.

Thank you, Lord, for all these sources of sunshine for a woman—all these ways to feel and celebrate spring.

God's name is worth honoring in a life that is worth living.

C. A. ROBERTS

Week 9

MARJORIE HOLMES
Lord, Let Me Love

For flowers that bloom
    about our feet;
For tender grass, so fresh
    and sweet;
For song of bird and hum
    of bee;
For all things fair we
    hear or see
Father in Heaven,
    we thank Thee!

RALPH WALDO
EMERSON

Life Out of Death

❧

They shall call His name Immanuel,
which is translated, "God with us."

MATTHEW 1:23

After the Crucifixion came the Resurrection. After the Resurrection the Ascension. Because Jesus wore a crown of thorns, He now wears a crown of glory. Because He became poor, He now sits enthroned. Because He made Himself of no reputation, He now has a name which is above every name. Because He was willing to become a slave, He is now Master of everything. Because He was obedient to death, He is Lord of Life and holds the keys of hell and of death. Because He made Himself of no reputation, every knee will some day bow before Him. Every renunciation led to glory.

Christ came first and foremost to those who have no hope.

MAX
LUCADO

❧

God could not more fully and plainly show us the glorious truth of life out of death than in these paradoxes of Jesus' own life and death. Is it not clear to us that the sacrifice of Calvary was not a tragedy but the release of life and power?

Do we believe this? How hard it is to believe that our own self-offering to Him will work in the same way. How easy it is for most of us to live as though we do not believe it.

ELISABETH ELLIOT
The Path of Loneliness

He Did It for You

·············· ❧ ··············

All things were made through Him, and without
Him nothing was made that was made.

JOHN 1:3

Why did God do it? A shack would have sufficed, but he gave us a mansion. Did he have to give the birds a song and the mountains a peak? Was he required to put stripes on the zebra and the hump on the camel? Would we have known the difference had he made the sunsets gray instead of orange? . . . Why wrap creation in such splendor? Why go to such trouble to give such gifts?

Why do you? You do the same. I've seen you searching for a gift. I've seen you stalking the malls and walking the aisles. I'm not talking about the obligatory gifts. I'm not describing the last-minute purchase of drugstore perfume on the way to the birthday party. Forget blue-light specials and discount purchases; I'm talking about that extra-special person and that extra-special gift. . . .Why do you do it? You do it so the eyes will pop. You do it so the heart will stop. You do it to hear those words of disbelief, "You did this for *me*?"

That's why you do it. And that is why God did it. Next time a sunrise steals your breath or a meadow of flowers leaves you speechless, remain that way. Say nothing and listen as heaven whispers, "Do you like it? I did it just for you."

MAX LUCADO
The Great House of God

God's Kingdom Stars

Those who are wise shall shine like the brightness of the firmament, and those who turn many to righteousness like the stars forever and ever.

DANIEL 12:3

*H*ave you noticed how Americans have gone star struck? Our appetite to know more about the lives of the rich and famous seems to be insatiable. We are obsessed with faces of movie stars and inquiry into their private lives. Talk shows, news programs, women's and even news magazines seem to be moving further from true journalism and more toward fluff about the famous.

What's happening to us, anyway? Have we given up *real* life in order to take on *reel* life? It seems like we all wish we were stars.

Did you ever wonder what it would be like to be one? Well, you are! You are God's kingdom star. You may be overweight, sport age spots, find a new crinkle in your face now and then. None of that matters. For your beauty is generated from the inside.

There is divine purpose in bringing out the best in one another.

DENIS
WAITLEY

BARBARA JOHNSON
Joy Breaks

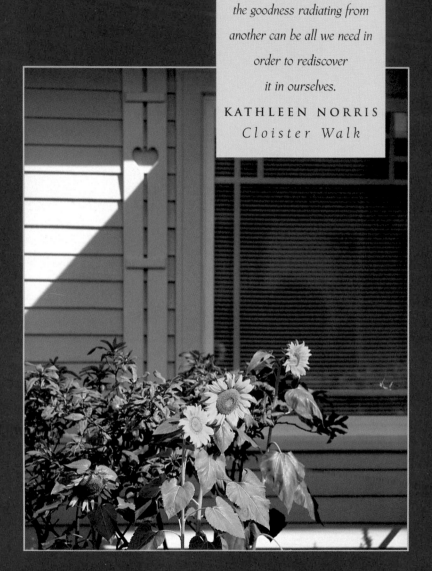

When we're at low ebb,
sometimes just to see
the goodness radiating from
another can be all we need in
order to rediscover
it in ourselves.

KATHLEEN NORRIS
Cloister Walk

Random Acts of Kindness

*This is My commandment, that you love
one another as I have loved you.*

JOHN 15:12

There is much more to hospitality than merely entertaining friends for dinner. Entertainment is only a part of what hospitality can offer. The woman who bathed Jesus' feet with ointment and kisses extended hospitality to Jesus that went well beyond entertainment. She was praised for her great love, which caused her to lavish such attention on Jesus. Like the woman at the Pharisee's house, when we practice hospitality we offer the gift of ourselves to friends, family, strangers, and even enemies.

Sometimes I think the closest most of us can ever come to expressing unconditional, *agape* love is through practicing hospitality with simple acts of kindness. . . .

Genuine hospitality is made up of random acts of kindness expressing Christ's grace and acceptance to whomever God puts in our lives. . . .

No one can "own" kindness. Like Christ's love, it is given with no strings attached. Even minuscule acts of kindness are released into the hands of our good God, who does what he wills without first checking in with us.

The opposite of availability is not unavailability, but an overcrowded heart.

SUE
MONK
KIDD

HARRIET CROSBY
A Place Called Home

Notes

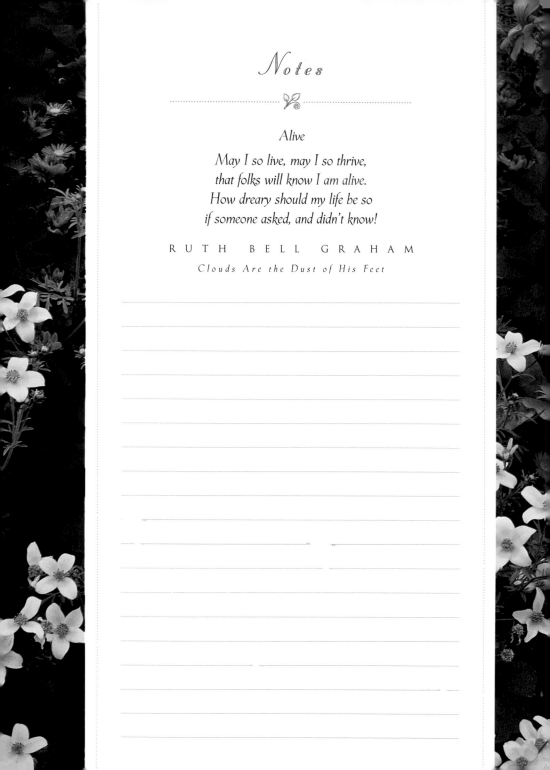

Alive

May I so live, may I so thrive,
that folks will know I am alive.
How dreary should my life be so
if someone asked, and didn't know!

RUTH BELL GRAHAM

Clouds Are the Dust of His Feet

Today Is Mine

❧

Looking unto Jesus, the author and finisher of our faith. . . .
HEBREWS 12:2

Sitting one still and sunny afternoon in a tiny chapel on an island in the South, I thought I heard someone enter. A young woman was weeping quietly. After a little time I asked if I could help. She confided her fears for the future—what if her husband should die? Or one of her children? What if money ran out?

All our fears represent in some form, I believe, the fear of death, common to all of us. But is it our business to pry into what may happen tomorrow? It is a difficult and painful exercise which saps the strength and uses up the time given us *today*. Once we give ourselves up to God, shall we attempt to get hold of what can never belong to us—tomorrow? Our lives are His, our times in His hand, He is Lord over what *will* happen, never mind what *may* happen. . . .

Today is mine. Tomorrow is none of my business. If I peer anxiously into the fog of the future, I will strain my spiritual eyes so that I will not see clearly what is required of me now.

When we come to the end of ourselves, we come to the beginning of God.

BILLY GRAHAM

❧

ELISABETH ELLIOT
Keep a Quiet Heart

The wind is a rollicking peddler,
crying his wonderful wares,
browbeating the world to buy.

I love your spring wind,
Lord, . . . its bright prancing.
It makes me want to dance too,
to roll a hoop, throw confetti,
gather armloads of flowers.

MARJORIE
HOLMES

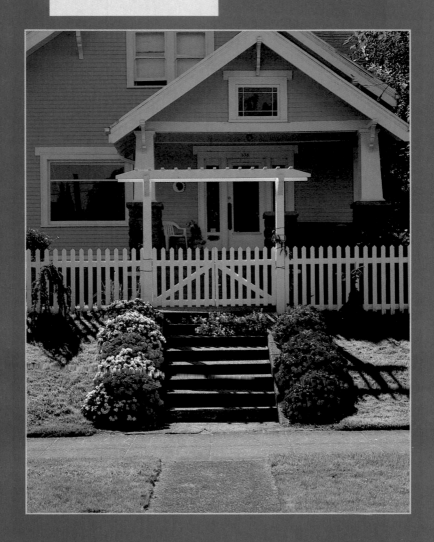

A Spring of Living Water

He will teach us His ways, and we shall walk in His paths.

MICAH 4:2

On the bank beside the road going up the mountain where I grew up, there is a freshwater spring. My mother had it dug out, lined with rocks, and then had a pipe put into it. To this day, the water flows from the spring, through the pipe, into an old oak bucket that then fills up with fresh spring water. . . .

On occasion, a small pebble or leaf or salamander gets lodged in the pipe, slowing or stopping the flow of the water into the bucket. Mother then runs a slender stick through the pipe to dislodge the blockage so the water can once again run freely.

Our lives are like that oak bucket, connected to the living Water of the Holy Spirit by our personal relationship with God through faith in Jesus Christ. When the Holy Spirit lives within us and we are totally yielded to Him, we are filled with living Water to the extent that we overflow into the lives of those around us.

But if something hinders our relationship with God, the flow of the Holy Spirit in and through our lives is blocked. . . . Like the blockage in the pipe, the sin must be removed, confessed specifically, then we must repent of the sin before the Holy Spirit is free once again to fill us up to overflow.

The essential part of Christian holiness is giving the heart wholly to God.

JOHN WESLEY

Week 10

ANNE GRAHAM LOTZ
The Vision of His Glory

> *We all take different roads home. Each of us is heading for the same destination, but we face our own variety of twists and turns and narrow places, as well as a few stretches that are all downhill.*
>
> JANET PASCHAL
> *The Good Road*

God's Kids

❧

But he who glories, let him glory in the LORD.

2 CORINTHIANS 10:17

Someone has said that when childhood dies, its corpses are called adults. Research shows that children laugh about four hundred times a day. How many times do you think adults have a good chuckle? Half that many? Or if you're more skeptical, a third as much? Wrong. Adults laugh only about fifteen times a day. That means adults laugh once for every twenty-six times a child has the same pleasure. Somewhere between childhood and maturity, things no longer seem so funny.

Why is that? Could it be that as we accumulate the experiences of crisis, disappointment, and stress, the delightful "why's?" of childhood—Why is the sky blue? Why do the birds sing?—become the "why me's?" that rob us of laughter and delight? . . .

Jesus told us to receive forgiveness for past sins and refuse to worry about tomorrow. In this way, living fully in the present moment, we become more like children with hearts open for laughter and joy.

Joy is the gigantic secret of the Christian.

G. K.
CHESTERTON

❧

BARBARA JOHNSON
Joy Breaks

Preparing the Heart for Fruit

❧

As far as the east is from the west, so far has
He removed our transgressions from us.

PSALM 103:12

Confession does for the soul what preparing the land does for the field. Before the farmer sows the seed he works the acreage, removing the rocks and pulling the stumps. He knows that seed grows better if the land is prepared. Confession is the act of inviting God to walk the acreage of our hearts. "There is a rock of greed over here Father, I can't budge it. And that tree of guilt near the fence? Its roots are long and deep. And may I show you some dry soil, too crusty for seed?" God's seed grows better if the soil of the heart is cleared.

And so the Father and the Son walk the field together; digging and pulling, preparing the heart for fruit. Confession invites the Father to work the soil of the soul.

MAX LUCADO
In the Grip of Grace

Humdudgeons or Contentment?

*Everywhere and in all things I have learned both to be full
and to be hungry, both to abound and to suffer need.*

PHILIPPIANS 4:12

The word *humdudgeon* is a new one to me, and I like the sound of it. It means "a loud complaint about a trifle." Heard any of those lately around your house? One mother thought of an excellent antidote: all humdudgeons must be presented not orally but in writing, "of two hundred words or more." There was a sudden marked reduction in whining and complaining.

Parents, by example, teach their children to whine. No wonder it is so difficult to teach them not to! Listen to conversations in the elevator, at the hairdresser's, at the next table in the restaurant.

Everybody's whining about everything—weather, health, the president, the IRS, the insurance mess, traffic, the kids. . . .

Everything about which we are tempted to complain may be the very instrument whereby the Potter intends to shape His clay into the image of His Son—a headache, an insult, a long line at the check-out, someone's rudeness or failure to say thank you, misunderstanding, disappointment, interruption. . . .

Wouldn't our children learn godliness if they saw the example of contentment instead of complaint? acceptance instead of rebellion? peace instead of frustration?

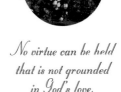

*No virtue can be held
that is not grounded
in God's love.*

RICHARD
MISYN

ELISABETH ELLIOT
Keep a Quiet Heart

No matter how uncertain
our world sometimes seems,
we can count on flowers
to appear each spring.

BARBARA MILO
OHRBACH

Simply Flowers

In the Kitchen with God

❧

Whatever your hand finds to do, do it with your might.

ECCLESIASTES 9:10

There's something about a kitchen
That unwinds taut springs of care—
A scented hustle-and-bustle
That begs contentment and prayer.

Only those who truly think of a kitchen as a laboratory of love can appreciate its pleasures. I believe that's the room where God and I have our best time together. We share the kitchen with no self-consciousness. I like to sing while I cook—especially the old songs—and if I clap when I get carried away on "Give Me That Old-Time Religion," nobody notices.

Countless analogies arise in a kitchen. Can you think of God as the leavening in the rising bread? Can you see His hand stamping "Grade A, Number 1" on our meat as He did for Moses? Can you see new life in the constant renewal of annuals that bloom along your window sill? Can you think of yourself feeding His sheep as He commanded Simon? Then, you are very blest. You are serving God and your family. How easy, relaxed, and natural it is to pray when one is performing a labor of love!

The more we get outside of self, the more we grow in Jesus.

WILLIAM
ROMAINE

❧

JUNE MASTERS BACHER
Quiet Moments for Women

Notes

Pippa's Song

The year's at the spring,
And day's at the morn;
Morning's at seven;
The hillside's dew-pearled;
The lark's on the wing;
The snail's on the thorn;
God's in His heaven—
All's right with the world!

ROBERT   BROWNING
1812 — 1889

Let Me Be Available

❧

*The LORD is good to all, and
His tender mercies are over all His works.*

Psalm 145:9

*As long as we can love
and pray, life has
charms for us.*

CHARLOTTE MARY
YONGE

❧

*J*esus didn't have a job with a myriad of tasks filling up at least eight hours a day, and he didn't have to commute. He didn't raise children, had no parent-teacher conferences to attend, no doctor and dentist appointments to arrange, no soccer games and piano lessons to drive to and sit through, no cars and appliances to repair.

But even if he had had to do all of those tasks, I have the feeling that he would have done them quite differently than I have. I can picture Jesus in line or in a waiting room, engaging someone near him in conversation rather than looking at his watch impatiently. On the sidelines of a soccer game, I'll bet he would be making new friends or deepening existing relationships. Driving his kids somewhere would provide an opportunity to be available to them and their friends in their excitement or apprehension about the events of their day. . . .

If our schedules are so cluttered that any surprise interruption is viewed as an unwelcome intrusion, we cannot practice the availability of Jesus.

JAMES MCGINNIS
"The Availability of Jesus"

The words "country flowers"
conjure up all the simple
varieties—cornfield poppies
and chamomile, deep blue
cornflowers and fat,
cabbagy roses.

LAURA ASHLEY

*"Flowers for All
Seasons"*

Hearts Set to Singing

⌇

Blessed are all who put their trust in Him.

Psalm 2:12

There is nothing haphazard about spring. It is not a fickle affair that happens some years and not others. Its advent is sure; its impact is enormous. Its coming produces incredible changes. It ushers in a wondrous regeneration of life.

For those of us sensitive in soul to the changes around us, spring spells liberty, freedom, and stimulation. Our spirits, attuned to the world around us, surge with new life. The urge to go out and explore, to hike, to climb a cliff, to roam at random, to wander free in the wind is a heady impulse that cannot be denied. Our hearts are set to singing. A bright light of excitement fills our eyes. Our muscles must move. Our strength must be spent in splendid exhilaration.

Though we scarcely seem to realize it, we too are being remade, quickened, reborn in resurrection life. The winter is past, the darkness is gone, the cold has vanished under the warming sun. And we are free, free, free!

Charity, like the sun, brightens every object on which it shines.

DANIEL
ORCUTT

⌇

Week 11

W. PHILLIP KELLER

Songs of My Soul

Morning is so new, unshabby
and unsoiled. Morning is like
a brand new garment fresh
out of the box. You want to
try it on. To wear it! No matter
what its color—sunny or
gray—garbed in morning
nothing seems impossible.

MARJORIE HOLMES
Lord, Let Me Love

Finding God's Grace

❧

*If we confess our sins, He is faithful and just to forgive us
our sins and to cleanse us from all unrighteousness.*

1 J O H N 1 : 9

*D*iscipline is easy for me to swallow. Logical to
assimilate. Manageable and appropriate. But
God's grace? Anything but. Examples?
How much time do you have?

David the psalmist becomes David the voyeur, but
by God's grace becomes David the psalmist again.

Peter denied Christ before he preached Christ.
Zacchaeus, the crook. The cleanest part of his life
was the money he'd laundered. But Jesus still had
time for him.

The thief on the cross: hell-bent and hung-out-to-
die one minute, heaven-bound and smiling the next.

Story after story. Prayer after prayer. Surprise after
surprise. Seems that God is looking more for ways to get us
home than for ways to keep us out. I challenge you to find one
soul who came to God seeking grace and did not find it.

*Our souls should be like
a clear glass through which
God can be seen.*

MOTHER
TERESA

❧

MAX LUCADO
When God Whispers Your Name

The Edge of Glory

❦

Whatever you do, do all to the glory of God.

1 CORINTHIANS 10:31

A picture hangs in my study. It is a wood-block print of a Celtic woman, dressed in the clothes of centuries ago, who has paused in her sweeping to bend over and examine the floor by candlelight. It is the artist's rendition of Jesus' parable of the lost coin. Printed next to the picture are the words of Esther de Waal: "She has made the mundane the edge of glory." The early Christian Celts believed all of what is life-giving to be seamless; there was no distinction between sacred and secular. They had a prayer for every activity, day or night. In Celtic spirituality ordinary life is suffused with the light of the glory of God. The picture reminds me that it simply takes prayer to catch a glimpse of the holy—and to rest in the glory of God.

"Do not worry about anything, but in everything by prayer and supplication with thanksgiving let your requests be made known to God. And the peace of God, which surpasses all understanding, will guard your hearts and your minds in Christ Jesus." (Philippians 4:6–7)

HARRIET CROSBY
A Place Called Home

God's Hot Water

❧

Peace I leave with you, My peace I give to you;
not as the world gives do I give to you.

JOHN 14:27

Recently I spoke at the Raisin Festival in Dinuba, California, the Raisin Capital of the World. I learned a lot about raisins there and watched how they turn grapes into raisins that are juicy and sweet. . . .

First, they take only the best California grapes. Then they give them the "spa treatment": the grapes are bathed in hot water followed by twenty-four hours of controlled dehydration in warm air. Finally, the raisins are cooled and gently washed again in warm water before being bundled in convenient packages. The process entails great care heating the initial hot-water bath, gradually cooling the water, then heating it again to insure plump, moist raisins.

I don't know about you, but I sure don't want to end up an old pious prune. Nor do I want to end up like one of those hard little crusty raisins I sometimes find at the bottom of a box. I'll gladly take the hot water God puts me in because I know *he* knows I need it. Sometimes a good soaking brings out stuff I didn't know I had in me, like courage, dignity, compassion.

Buried under the biggest burden is a good place to find an ever bigger blessing.

JANETTE OKE

❧

BARBARA JOHNSON
Joy Breaks

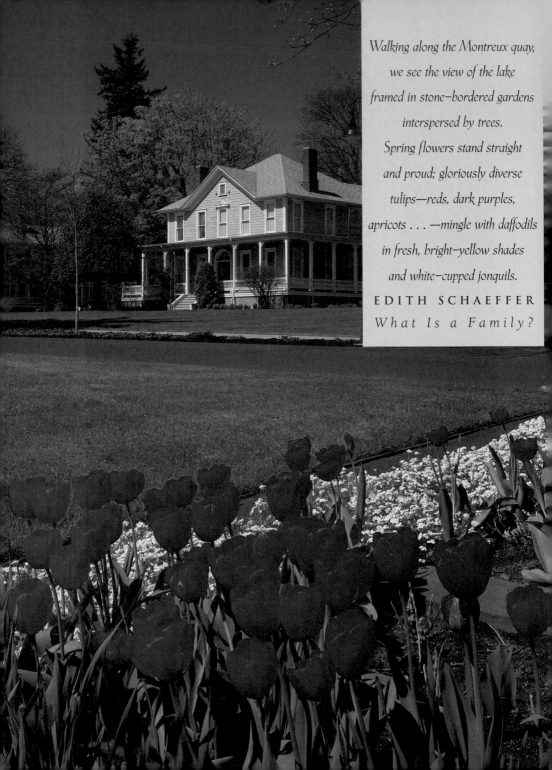

Walking along the Montreux quay,
we see the view of the lake
framed in stone-bordered gardens
interspersed by trees.
Spring flowers stand straight
and proud; gloriously diverse
tulips—reds, dark purples,
apricots . . . —mingle with daffodils
in fresh, bright-yellow shades
and white-cupped jonquils.

EDITH SCHAEFFER
What Is a Family?

Persistent Prayer

And whatever things you ask in prayer, believing, you will receive.

MATTHEW 21:22

G od can change our circumstances, but sometimes He waits for us to show real desire for change as well as our faith in Him. . . . How do you and I show our eagerness to receive all that God has promised us? One way is through persistent prayer as we ask God for change and seek His Word about the change then persistently and respectfully pray until He brings it about. . . .

The Korean church is known around the world for being a praying church. Korean Christians pray and fast on specially designated mountains for days, weeks, and even months. Literally hundreds and thousands of Christians attend daily prayer sessions at 4:30 A.M. One old Korean lady who attended the early-morning prayer meeting every day always put her husband's empty shoes on the front pew of the church, saying, "Here are my husband's shoes, Lord. I believe one day my husband will be here to fill them." One year after she began demonstrating this confident hope by bringing her husband's shoes to the prayer service, the shoes were filled! Her husband came with her and placed his faith in Jesus Christ as his Lord and Savior.

What "shoes" do you have to put before the Lord?

Confident expectation should keep pace with earnest supplication.

C. H.
SPURGEON

ANNE GRAHAM LOTZ
The Glorious Dawn of God's Story

Notes

Father, let our faithful mind
Rest, on Thee alone inclined;
Every anxious thought repress,
Keep our souls in perfect peace.

CHARLES WESLEY

Lord of the Sabbath

❧

He has put a new song in my mouth—praise to our God.

PSALM 40:3

*A spirit of calm contentment
always accompanies
true godliness.*

ELISABETH
ELLIOT

❧

*S*o the week has been overwhelming? You want a sanitized house. Your family deserves nutritious meals. Your job is demanding (whether you are an office slave or a house hold servant!). You would like to take an art course, write a poem, create a garden, maybe take a trip . . .

"I can't do it all!" you screamed above the hiss of the shower over and over when you were alone half a blissful moment.

Of course, you can't. Don't you think God knew that? That's why He created Sundays. Now the helter-skelter existence will commence anew on Monday. But maybe you can face life a day at a time if you use today wisely breathing in God in big, big doses.

Normally, when the channels get clogged, you have to kneel in a wee chapel inside your heart. [In the Scriptures we find] the Sabbath referred to as: 1. a blessed and holy rest day (meaning *happy* and *set apart*); 2. a day of deliverance (you need it!); 3. a day of delight (haven't you escaped bondage?); and 4. a day made for us. Christ is Lord of the Sabbath. He wants it restful, peaceful, and *healing*.

JUNE MASTERS BACHER
The Quiet Heart

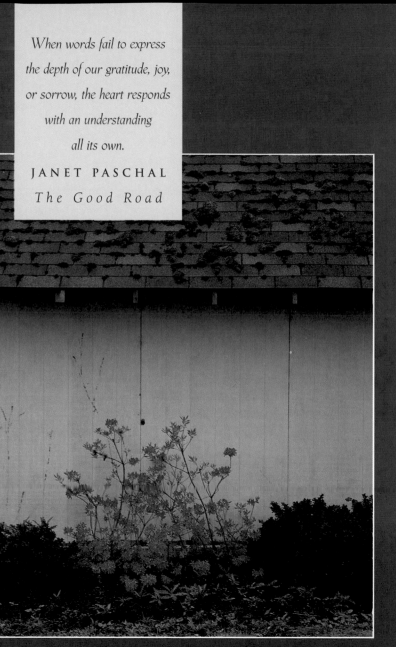

When words fail to express the depth of our gratitude, joy, or sorrow, the heart responds with an understanding all its own.

JANET PASCHAL
The Good Road

My Garden

*I will look to the LORD; I will wait for the God
of my salvation; my God will hear me.*

MICAH 7:7

This is my garden, God, this is my garden, my own small precious portion of the earth that you have made.

I will dig and hoe and tend it, I will grub in the soil that is cool and moist and scented with spring.

I will find you in that soil as I crumble its clods or press these small seeds deep into its dark flesh.

What a joyful thing, the feel of your silent soil. . . .It receives my little offerings—these tiny plants, these slips and cuttings, these infinitesimal seedlings, with a kind of blind, uncommenting magnificence. I am a trifle awed before it, I am filled with an amused humility.

May I never seek in the creature what can be found only in the Creator.

PURITAN
PRAYER

How insignificant I am that I should be entrusted with this miracle to come. No, no, the earth will surely reject my anxious efforts, my foolish hopes. Yet I know a happy patience too. Wait—only wait upon the Lord, as the Bible says.

Week 12

And sure enough. The silent, teeming forces of creation set to work, and soon the miracle has come! Onions and lettuce for the table. Shrubs to be trimmed. The incredible colors and fragrances of flowers.

MARJORIE HOLMES
Lord, Let Me Love

*Spring blossoms herald
a rich harvest throughout
summer and autumn.
Few other foods provide
such spectacular range
of intense tastes and colors as
the fruits of the orchard trees,
soft-fruit canes and bushes,
and the tangled branches
of the hedgerows.*

HENRIETTA GREEN

*A Glorious
Harvest*

The Plague of Worry

.... ✧ ....

And he said, "My presence will go with you and I will give you rest."

EXODUS 33:14

Worry," says Vance Havner "is like sitting in a rocking chair. It will give you something to do, but it won't get you anywhere." Worry and anxiety have hounded the human race since the beginning of time, and modern man with all his innovations has not found the cure for the plague of worry.

Physicians tell us that 70 percent of all illnesses are imaginary, the cause being mental distress or worry. . . .

Psychiatrists tell us that worry breeds nervous breakdowns and mental disorders. . . .

What is the answer? The hymn-writer, Edward Henry Bickersteth, hinted at it when he wrote: "Peace, perfect peace, in this dark world of sin? The blood of Jesus whispers peace within."

I have cast my anchor in the port of peace, knowing that present and future are in nail-pierced hands.

PURITAN
PRAYER

The sea was beating against the rocks in huge, dashing waves. The lightning was flashing, the thunder was roaring, the wind was blowing; but the little bird was asleep in the crevice of the rock, its head serenely under its wing, sound asleep. That is peace—to be able to sleep in the storm! In Christ, we are relaxed and at peace in the midst of the confusions, bewilderments, and perplexities of this life. The storm rages, but our hearts are at rest.

BILLY GRAHAM
Unto the Hills

The Perfume of Love

.... ✣ ....

He who does good is of God, but he who does evil has not seen God.

3 JOHN 11

One of my dear friends is an elderly widow who lives in an austere retirement center in the very heart of the city. Endless traffic and crowds of pedestrians press in around her residence in a constant cacophony of noise and confusion. The halls she walks are dim, dark, haunted by aged people who for the most part have given up hope. Her own tiny room is almost like a narrow cell with a limited outlook between the building's concrete walls.

Yet in such a stark setting this loving lady pours out the perfume of her gracious personality upon every life she touches. Every day she is fit enough to get out, she takes walks to pick any stray flowers, or leaves, or even decorative wayside weeds she can find. These she brings back to share with others who are shut-ins or others in the hospital. . . . Her tiny figure is filled with laughter, fun, and the joyous optimism of one who loves her Father and revels in His company. The sunshine of the sky, the wonder of the stars, the fragrance of flowers, the healing touch of trees and grass are reflected in the gentle love pouring from the soul and spirit of this saint.

Wherever she goes, she leaves behind a legacy of hope, of cheer, of good will to those she meets. Through her little life there radiates to all around her the character of Christ, the gentle glory of God.

W. PHILLIP KELLER
Songs of My Soul

One Day at a Time

❧

Your Father knows the things you have need of before you ask Him.

MATTHEW 6:8

When was the last time you thanked the Lord for not showing you the future? I'm convinced that one of the best things God does for us is to keep us from knowing what will happen beyond today. Just think of all the stuff you didn't have to worry about just because you never knew it was coming your way!

It's true, God never changes . . . but we certainly do. The places we live change. People change. Even friends change. Jobs change.

Or how about your home? Things change there, too. Children are conceived unexpectedly. Many parents are brokenhearted because their older children are not walking with God. Others are sorrowing because death has taken a parent or a son or daughter. Our health changes. Or how about tests in life? Just think of what has happened in the past five years. Aren't you glad God didn't tell you about all of those things *five years ago*? Aren't you glad He didn't give you your life ahead of time, on credit? Instead, we just take life one day at a time. That's the way He dispenses life. Because He never changes and He knows what will work together for good. You and I don't.

Faith is what you have in the absence of knowledge.

FLANNERY O'CONNOR

❧

CHARLES SWINDOLL
David: A Man of Passion and Destiny

Wrens and robins in the hedge.
Wrens and robins here
and there; Building, perching,
pecking, fluttering, Everywhere!

C H R I S T I N A
R O S S E T T I

The Sin Stain

❧

You have forgiven the iniquity of Your people;
You have covered all their sin.

PSALM 85:2

Blessed Holy Spirit, melt
my heart by the majesty
and mercy of God.

PURITAN
PRAYER

❧

Many of the later–model cars are equipped with theft alarm systems. The more sensitive ones can be annoying to the general public as the least bit of motion by a passer–by or the lightest touch to the car body can send off an ear–splitting siren, accompanied by flashing lights and honking horn. But that obnoxious sensitivity is purposefully designed to be a protection against unwanted entry.

God has built into each of us an alarm system to warn us of the unwanted entry of sin into our lives. The alarm system is called *guilt*. Guilt is our friend. Without it we would go on in sin until we were dominated and defeated by it.

In our pleasure–seeking, anything–goes, feel–good society, guilt is anathema. We run from it through frantic activity, drown it in alcohol, drug it with Prozac, escape it through entertainment, talk about it to a therapist, blame it on someone else, suppress it through mental gymnastics, but we can't rid ourselves of it! It's like a stain that won't come out of our clothes no matter how many wash cycles we put it through or what kind of detergent we use! . . . The *only* thing that can "wash away" our sin and guilt before God is the blood of Jesus Christ.

ANNE GRAHAM LOTZ
The Glorious Dawn of God's Story

Notes

I conclude that, for me, there is no other way but to walk with Christ—to study Him, to pursue Him. He has carved a place in my heart that yearns for Him.

JANET PASCHAL
The Good Road

Solitude in the Garden

❧

Search me, O God, and know my heart;
try me and know my anxieties.

PSALM 139:23

A friend commented once that she went through her days taking imaginary pictures, snapshots of the important moments, and it was essential to her health and well-being that she take the time at some point to sort through the photos. If she couldn't carve out time during the day, then her mind insisted on it at night. . . .

For those seeking to deepen our lives in Christ, to bring all of our lives before Him, reflection is necessary. To carry the analogy further, we must sit with Him in a garden of solitude, showing Him the snapshots of our daily lives and discussing them with Him, asking what they mean, what He wants to show us. . . .

The point is this. Often, if we barrel through our days with no reflection and without listening to God's voice in the middle of the bustling, niggling, babbling pother, then we miss both His presence (an enormous gift in itself), and we miss His other gifts bestowed on us simply because we are alive on the earth. . . . We are considerably poorer if we do not take the time to be with God in the garden.

Give yourself to God to be what He wills you to be.

DAVID
LIVINGSTONE

❧

LESLIE WILLIAMS
Night Wrestling

How impudent are morning birds!
Trilling and cheeping and shrilling
their glad little cries.
Running scales. Ringing bells
of brightness. Chiming.

MARJORIE HOLMES
Lord, Let Me Love

The Tapestry of Our Lives

❧

You are my hiding place and my shield; I hope in Your word.

PSALM 119:114

My life has included sorrow as well as happiness. And all those emotions, all those bittersweet memories, have created what I like to think of as a bright, colorful, firmly woven tapestry.

The happy times are the golden threads that catch the sunlight, warming the soul. The bright pattern was created by our children and then the grandchildren, whose sparkling threads added a nubby texture, a splash of vivid color, to the fabric. The black, somber woof threads that subdue the tapestry's gaudiness were painstakingly woven as we endured hardships in life.

The Lord is my strength to climb the Hill of Difficulty and not be afraid.

LETTIE B. COWMAN

❧

Some of the threads in my tapestry are frayed. Others are broken. But the tapestry remains intact because other threads, as invisible as love yet as strong as the everlasting arms, are woven amongst the weakened ones, holding the delicate fibers together.

As I reminisce, I think of

Week 13

how we wove our way through joys and sorrow, good times and bad, glorying in each other's triumphs and supporting each other in times of trial. And in every loop and knot of our lives together, I see the hand of God.

BARBARA JOHNSON
Living Somewhere Between Estrogen and Death

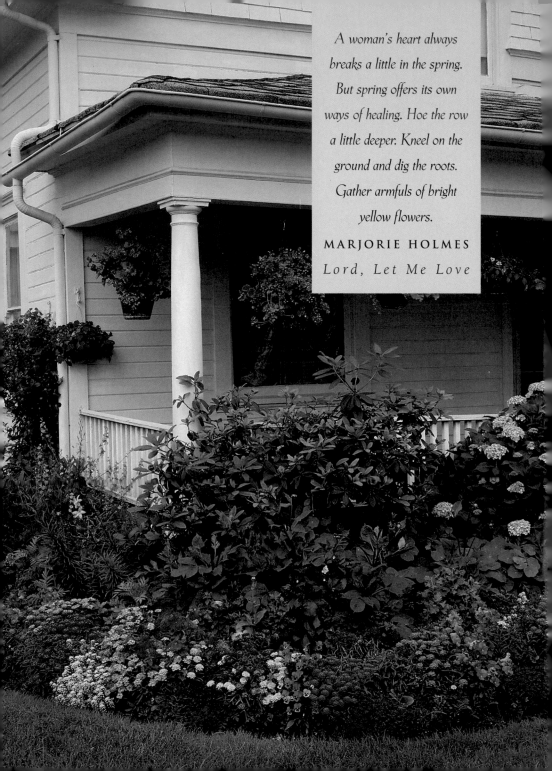

A woman's heart always breaks a little in the spring. But spring offers its own ways of healing. Hoe the row a little deeper. Kneel on the ground and dig the roots. Gather armfuls of bright yellow flowers.

MARJORIE HOLMES

Lord, Let Me Love

Inner Beauty

❧

You are my hiding place and my shield; I hope in Your word.

PSALM 119:114

When the Master Potter shapes us for His service, He is concerned that we do not become proud of our own beauty, of our intellectual gifts, of our education and achievements. When we are on display in the world, those watching us need to become more excited about the power of God working through us than about who we are. . . .

An experience I had during the second World War illustrates how unimportant our exterior display is when the heart is right. I was sitting in the bulkhead seat of an airplane going from Chicago to California. In the seat next to me was Eleanor Roosevelt. In my weakness, and because of Hollywood's influence, when I looked at her I thought, *She is so homely.* But then I started talking with her, and she started asking me questions. Out of her eyes came such caring concern that I was overwhelmed. She had a sweetness and a caring that just spilled out—and she was not unattractive anymore.

I was reading a prayer book at the time, so I asked her to sign the flyleaf—one of only two people I have ever asked for an autograph.

People who make a difference can be stretched, pulled, pushed, and changed.

CHARLES R. SWINDOLL

❧

DALE EVANS ROGERS
In the Hands of the Potter

Distorting the Truth

❧

*Trust in the LORD and do good; dwell in the land,
and feed on His faithfulness.*

PSALM 37:3

We live in a world that lies to us every single day. It's a consequence of living in a world that has turned its back on the Source of truth. Every day, women in our society are told in a thousand different ways that to be lovable, they must be beautiful. The message they receive is that the catalyst for lasting, fulfilling relationships is physical appearance. And although few women would admit they buy into that line of thinking, fewer still could deny having acted on it. . . .

Repeated exposure to the lies of this world takes its toll. Over time, these lies are woven into the fabric of our thinking. We aren't always aware that they're there. Often we are unaware of the ideas that form the basis of our decisions and attitudes. But these beliefs, whether grounded in reality or not, act as the grid system through which we interpret the data of our lives. . . .

Wherever there is a distortion of the truth, eventually, it is reflected in our behavior. . . . Until you deal with your belief system, your behavior will never change because what you believe affects what you do.

ANDY STANLEY
Like a Rock

Prayer Is Asking

Whatever you ask in My name, that I will do,
that the Father may be glorified in the Son.

JOHN 14:13

How often Jesus prefaced some teaching to His big, burly disciples with an affectionate: "Little children, I tell you . . . ." And of course the characteristic position of childhood is that of simple asking.

A little child who has no shyness or hesitation about asking his parents for what he needs is unselfconsciously revealing his helplessness—along with a normal, right relationship with his father and mother. In the same way, asking immediately puts us into a right relationship to God. It is acting out the fact that He is the Creator with the riches and resources we need; we are the creatures who need help. It's a cap-in-hand stance. Which we resist because it diminishes us—a certain amount of pride and self has to go for us to ask for help—whether of God or of another human being. . . .

God insists that we ask, not because *He* needs to know our situation, but because *we* need the spiritual discipline of asking.

All the imbalances have come as a result of sin upsetting the perfect balance.

EDITH
SCHAEFFER

CATHERINE MARSHALL
Adventures in Prayer

Perpetual springtime

is not allowed.

C. S. LEWIS

For Our Good and God's Glory

❦

Blessed is he whose transgression is forgiven, whose sin is covered.

PSALM 32:1

There is a well-known story of some men in Scotland who had spent the day fishing. That evening they were having tea in a little inn. One of the fishermen, in a characteristic gesture to describe the size of the fish that got away, flung out his hands just as the little waitress was getting ready to set the cup of tea at his place. The hand and the teacup collided, dashing the tea against the white-washed walls. Immediately an ugly brown stain began to spread over the wall. The man who did it was very embarrassed and apologized profusely, but one of the other guests jumped up and said, "Never mind." Pulling a pen from his pocket, he began to sketch around the ugly brown stain. Soon there emerged a picture of a magnificent royal stag with his antlers spread. That artist was Sir Edwin Landsee, England's foremost painter of animals.

This story has always beautifully illustrated to me the fact that if we confess not only our sins but our mistakes to God, He can make out of them something for our good and for His glory.

BILLY GRAHAM
Unto the Hills

Because all of us are born in sin, all of us are rebellious, some more than others.

ELISABETH
ELLIOT

❦

Notes

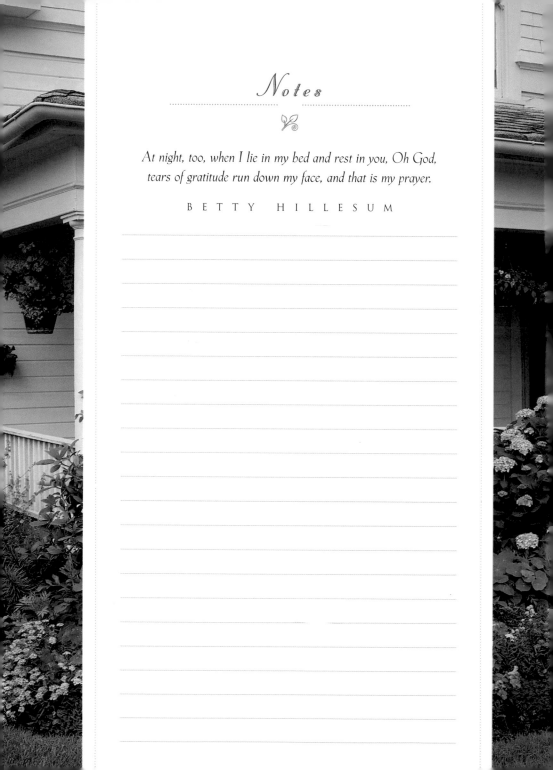

At night, too, when I lie in my bed and rest in you, Oh God,
tears of gratitude run down my face, and that is my prayer.

BETTY HILLESUM

A Home for Your Heart

❧

*Let the peace of God rule in your hearts, to which also
you were called in one body; and be thankful.*

COLOSSIANS 3:15

When it comes to resting your soul, there is no place like the Great House of God. "I'm asking Yahweh for one thing," [David] wrote, "only one thing: to live with him in his house my whole life long. I'll contemplate his beauty, I'll study at his feet. That's the only quiet secure place in a noisy world" (Ps. 27:4–5 MSG).

If you could ask God for one thing, what would you request? David tells us what he would ask. He longs to *live* in the house of God. I emphasize the word *live*, because it deserves to be emphasized. David doesn't want to chat. He doesn't desire a cup of coffee on the back porch. He doesn't ask for a meal or to spend an evening in God's house. He wants to move in with him . . . forever. He's asking for his own room . . . permanently. He doesn't want to be stationed in God's house, he longs to retire there. He doesn't seek a temporary assignment, but rather lifelong residence.

*Longing for God creates
an intensity of spirit.*

JOEL
GREGORY

❧

MAX LUCADO
The Great House of God

Acknowledgments

Grateful acknowledgment is made to the following publishers and copyright holders for permission to reprint copyrighted material.

June Masters Bacher, *Quiet Moments for Women* (Eugene, Or.: Harvest House, 1979). © Harvest House Publishers. Used by permission.

June Masters Bacher, *The Quiet Heart* (Eugene, Or.: Harvest House, 1988). © Harvest House Publishers. Used by permission.

Patsy Clairmont, Barbara Johnson, Marilyn Meberg, and Luci Swindoll. *Joy Breaks.*© 1997 by New Life Clinics. Used by permission of Zondervan Publishing House.

Harriet Crosby, *A Well-Watered Garden* (Nashville: Thomas Nelson, 1995).

Harriet Crosby, *A Place Called Home* (Nashville, Thomas Nelson, 1997).

Elisabeth Elliot, *The Path of Loneliness* (Nashville: Thomas Nelson, 1988).

Elisabeth Elliot, *Keep a Quiet Heart* (Ann Arbor, Mich.: Servant Books, 1995).

Elisabeth Elliot, *God's Guidance* (Grand Rapids: Fleming H. Revell, a division of Baker Book House 1997).

Elisabeth Elliot, *Discipline: the Glad Surrender* (Grand Rapids: Fleming H. Revell, a division of Baker Book House 1982).

Ruth Bell Graham, *Clouds Are the Dust of His Feet* (Wheaton, Ill.: Crossway Books, 1992). © Ruth Bell Graham.

Billy Graham, *Unto the Hills* (Dallas: Word, 1996).

Billy Graham, *The Secret of Happiness* (Dallas: Word, 1985).

Liz Curtis Higgs, *Reflecting His Image* (Nashville: Thomas Nelson, 1996).

Marjorie Holmes, *Lord, Let Me Love* (New York: Bantam Doubleday Dell, 1978). © Marjorie Holmes.

Wayne Jacobsen, *In My Father's Vineyard* (Dallas: Word, 1997).

Barbara Johnson, *Living Somewhere Between Estrogen and Death* (Dallas: Word, 1997).

Phillip Keller, *A Shepherd Looks at the Good Shepherd and His Sheep* (Dallas: Word, 1986).

Phillip Keller, *Songs of My Soul* (Dallas: Word, 1989).

Phillip Keller, *Taming Tension* (Grand Rapids: Baker Book House, 1979).

Heather Harpham Kopp, *Patchwork of Love* (Sisters, Or.: Multnomah Books, 1997). © by Multnomah Publishers, Used by permission.

Anne Graham Lotz, *The Vision of His Glory* (Dallas: Word, 1996).

Anne Graham Lotz, *The Glorious Dawn of God's Story* (Dallas: Word, 1997).

Max Lucado, *The Great House of God* (Dallas: Word, 1997).

Max Lucado, *In the Grip of Grace* (Dallas: Word, 1996).

Max Lucado, *When God Whispers Your Name* (Dallas: Word, 1994).

Catherine Marshall, *Adventures in Prayer* (Old Tappan, N.J.: Chosen Books, 1976). Used by permission of Baker Book House.

James McGinnis, "The Availability of Jesus," *Weavings*, vol. 12, no. 5, September/October 1997.

Janet Paschal, *The Good Road* (Sisters, Or.: Multnomah Books, 1997). © by Janet Paschal.

Stacy and Paula Rinehart, *Living in Light of Eternity* (Colorado Springs: NavPress, 1986).

Dale Evans Rogers, *In the Hands of the Potter* (Nashville: Thomas Nelson, 1994).

David Roper, *Psalm 23: Hope and Rest from the Shepherd* (Grand Rapids: Discovery House, 1994). © David Roper. Used by permission of Discovery House Publishers, Box 3566, Grand Rapids, MI 49501. All rights reserved.

Edith Schaeffer, *Common Sense Christian Living* (Nashville, Tenn.: Thomas Nelson, 1983).

Edith Schaeffer, *What Is a Family?* (Grand Rapids, Mich.: Baker Book House, 1975).

Robert Schuller, *Tough Times Never Last but Tough People Do* (Dallas: Word, 1983).

Soul Searching: Meditations for Your Spiritual Journey (Nashville: Thomas Nelson, 1995).

Andy Stanley, *Like a Rock: Becoming a Person of Character* (Nashville: Thomas Nelson, 1997).

Penelope J. Stokes, *Faith: The Substance of Things Unseen* (Wheaton: Tyndale, 1995). © Penelope J. Stokes.

Charles Swindoll, *David: A Man of Passion and Destiny* (Dallas: Word, 1997).

Charles Swindoll, *Simple Faith* (Dallas: Word, 1997).

Joni Eareckson Tada, *Diamonds in the Dust* (Grand Rapids; Zondervan, 1993). © by Joni Eareckson Tada. Used by permission of Zondervan Publishing House.

Mother Teresa, *The Love of Christ* (San Francisco, Harper & Row, 1982).

Leslie Williams, *Night Wrestling* (Dallas: Word, 1997).

Photo Credits

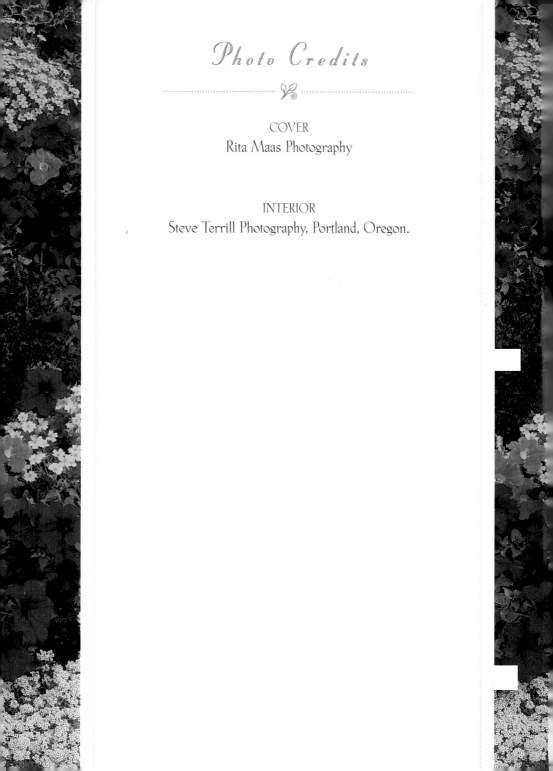

COVER
Rita Maas Photography

INTERIOR
Steve Terrill Photography, Portland, Oregon.